"An Exploration of Chaplaincy"

By Dr. Richard Mc Cready

Published by Papito Publishing Co.
Post Office Box 75535
Los Angeles, California 90005
(323) 702 1524 / (323) 559 0170
Http: \\ www. Papito.com/anoble@aol.com

ABSTRACT

Chaplains go where others would never consider! Never believe that a few kind and caring people cannot change the world. For in reality, they are the only ones who ever have.

Chaplain Charles Gibson, Chaplain Ministries

DEDICATION

This book is dedicated first of all to my dear wife, Clara, who instilled in me the need to pursue and further my education both in the spiritual as well as the secular arena.

In addition, this book is dedicated to the fallen Chaplains who gave their services willing and without preservation.

Finally, I dedicate this book to the men and women who serves daily to ensure that our fine law enforcement officers are acknowledged and spiritually represented.

ACKNOWLEDGEMENTS

I am grateful to Almighty God for having me pursue this project. I am especially indebted to my wife and family for their understanding and patience. Heart-felt thanks goes to Tanya Washington and Dr. Ligons, Dr. Butler and Dr. Miller for proofreading and editing the text. I thank all of those collaborators that contributed in whatever manner to bring this project to fruition.

I wish to thank Dr. Hall and Dr. Harden, for your encouragement and instructions; Dr. Noble, for your gracious words of contribution to this work.

Thank you Dr. Oath, my children: Richard McCready, Jr., Stephanie Bradley, Sherill Denise McCready, Marsha Renee Ellis. Terrie Lynn McCready, Dr. Trimble and Elder Wright for your patience, your service and forbearance you extended to me throughout this project and school year. I pray God will continue to bless you for your labor of love
.

FOREWORD

There is so little written about the LAPD Chaplain and their work. Certainly, libraries and religious bookstores have periodicals and clippings, but not detail concise works on the subject.

Pastor Richard McCready has been a viable Chaplain for the Newton Street Police Department and has firsthand knowledge and in-depth understanding to the needs of the officers and therefore is able to bring to light insight to what is little known about this great corps.

Those who would or have the desire to become more knowledgeable about the work of the Chaplain Corps should have a copy of this thesis in their collection.

Dr. Alfredo D. Noble, PhD

TABLE OF CONTENTS

COPYRIGHT   II

ABSTRACT   III

DEDICATION   IV

ACKNOWLEDGEMENTS   V

FOREWORD   VI

CHAPTERS

    I.   INTRODUCTION   1
            Background   2
            Objectives   3
            Methodology   3
                Organization of the Study   3
                    Research Questions   3
                    Definitions   4

    II.   LITERATURE REVIEW   7
                Sociological Challenges and Chaplain
            Ministry   8
                Health Care   8
                Military   9
                Parliamentary   12
                Law Enforcement   12
                Fire Department   14
                Corporate   15
                Sports   15

Domestic	**15**
Educational Institutions	**17**
Other	**18**

III.   THE IMPORTANCE OF COUNSELING OTHERS   19

IMPORTANCE OF THE ROLE OF MILITARY CHAPLAINS AND OTHER CLERGY IN SERVING VICTIMS OF CRIME   20

IV.   WORDS OF ASSURANCE   55
1. **Description of Interview Questions** 44
2. **Role of Interviewer** 56
3. **Protection Methods Utilized** 46
4. **Summation** 55
5. **Other Pertinent Information** 56

V.   SUMMARY & CONCLUSIONS   104
1. **Overview of Findings** 106
2. **Biblical Perspectives** 107
3. **Suggestions for Further Research** 119
4. **Research Questions** 119
5. **Definitions** 119

Epilogue	**132**
References	**133**
Appendixes	**137**
VITA	**151**

"An Exploration of Chaplaincy"

CHAPTER 1

AN EXPLORATION OF CHAPLAINCY

INTRODUCTION:

In fulfillment of my graduate research project, this researcher will explore the chaplaincy ministry, the role of the chaplain, the types of chaplains and how one becomes a chaplain. Through this work, an effort will be made to create awareness to the ministry of the chaplain. This research will also explore scriptural foundation for this ministry outside the typical religious institution, such as a church or mission, to meet needs of people in crisis.

Central to this thesis is the proposition that although public awareness has increased in recent years, many local churches (clergy) are far from understanding the ministry of chaplaincy – there should be an urgency to understand this ministry and its contribution to mankind, men and women can be reached and positively impacted by the chaplaincy.

David B. Plummer, in his book, *Just What is Chaplaincy*, explains that, the chaplain does not minister to a congregation, but to the public at large; the people who make up this chaplaincy community may wear hospital gowns, military uniforms, hard hats or orange jumpsuits. He goes on to say that like the Apostle Paul, chaplains are usually "tent-makers" and minister to people in crisis. Many people in need may never walk through the doors of a church, talk with a minister or become a member of an organized congregation, known as the church, mission or synagogue.

It is essential for chaplains to work outside of a religious institution to minister to the spiritual needs of mankind. Believers are given a mandate to "Go ye therefore, and teach all nations …" (Matthew 28:19 KJV) Workers are needed in the vineyard. "The harvest is truly plenteous but the laborers are few;" (Matthew 9:37 KJV). This researcher shall examine the chaplaincy ministry and the role, types, benefits and challenges within the scope of chaplaincy.

The Holy Bible teaches to encourage, aid your fellow man – meeting the needs of others.

Where people are spiritually, mentally, physically and emotionally, they sometimes need help to bring them to a place of peace.

My desire for this project is to create a new awareness of chaplaincy and to inspire the embrace of the role of the chaplain.

BACKGROUND:

While shopping at a large department store in Long Beach, California, I certainly was not thinking about how to become a chaplain, chaplain training, a chaplain career or anything related to chaplaincy. But in late October of 2000, a man who had been a pastor with me for a number of years saw me shopping. Truth be told, we were both victims of pastor burnout, but neither of us used that term nor did we see the positives and negative pastoral problems. Our meeting would have huge implications in changing the direction of my career, becoming a "change career, with purpose" encounter.

We chatted for a few minutes catching up on each other's lives. We discovered that we lived six blocks from one another! In early January 2001 he called me and said he must talk to me and that it was urgent. Our meeting would impact my ministry career and would start me thinking about how to become a chaplain, lead me to a life changing chaplain training opportunity, resulting in people addressing me as Chaplain Robert as I began my chaplain career.

Throughout the Bible, God used His Prophets and leaders to deliver His messages and to encourage His people through His Word. Jesus himself was the ultimate example of compassion. Whether it was the fisherman by the seashore, a woman at a well, a persecutor on the road to Damascus, a man in the belly of a whale or even the persecutor at His crucifixion, he always took time for people in crisis. We are all endowed with gifts or talents.

Therefore, whether it is in the organized setting of a congregation, a mission, synagogue, or a hospital, jail, battle field or work place, when there is need for spiritual wellness, there is a need for someone of faith to reach out to minister to people in crisis. Just as lay counselors are extensions of pastoral care in the local church, the chaplain is the extension of the clergy in places where the pastor cannot be, could not go and sometimes would not be received to meet the needs of people in crisis. So goes the ministry of chaplaincy.

<u>OBJECTIVES</u>:
Clearly define "chaplaincy" and "chaplain" and other uncommon terms relating to the subject.
Clarify and define the role of the chaplain and the types of chaplains.
Provide Scriptural references that support the work of the chaplain in offering strength, hope, assurance, courage and promises.
Highlight certain chaplains by name and present their contribution(s).

<u>METHODOLOGY</u>:
In addition to special academic research this researcher may conduct interviews with members of the law enforcement community who are willing to discuss

their interest and concerns regarding the chaplain in law enforcement. Interviews will be scheduled and conducted only after the "list" of questions have been submitted to and approved by Dr. Ernest Miller, Academic Dean at Long Beach Bible College.   All information given will be handled confidentially, and the identity of the interviewees will not be revealed (upon requested). The following questions were used:

What do think of the chaplains' role in your department?
What about the chaplains you have in your department?
When it comes to the tragic things of the community; how can we [community, clergy, etc.] be a help in that way?
What life events led you to become a chaplain?
Did you attend a house of worship throughout your childhood?
What part of your job do you struggle with emotionally?
What part of your job brings you the most joy?
What makes you cry?
What frustrates and/or angers you?
What kind of education and training do you have that enables you to perform in this capacity?
What would you say to others considering Chaplaincy as a profession?
What is the role of a chaplain apart from the armed forces or institution and what is that chaplain's role between communities and police department?

DEFINITIONS:

What is a chaplain? A chaplain as defined by Wisegeek "is a member of the clergy who works in a lay, or non-religious, institution, such as an army, a prison, a hospital, or a university. Other members of the clergy typically work in a church or mission setting. Lay chaplains, who minister but are not ordained, are becoming increasingly common. The term *lay minister* or *lay clergy* may also be used for chaplains who are ordained to indicate that they work outside of a religious institution; however, this use of the term is no longer common." (Wisegeek, 2003)

A **chaplain** is typically a priest, pastor, ordained deacon, rabbi, imam, other member of the clergy, or another representative of a faith or belief, serving a group of people who are not organized as a mission or church, or who are unable to attend religious services for various reasons, such as health, confinement, or military or civil duties. Lay chaplains are also found in other settings such as universities. For example, a chaplain is often attached to a military unit (where he or she is sometimes referred to as *padre*), a private chapel, a ship, a prison, a hospital, a high school, college or especially boarding school, a parliamentary assembly and so on. Though originally the word, chaplain, had Christian roots, it is now applied to men or women of other religions -- and sometimes, to individuals claiming no religion, as in the case of the humanist chaplains serving with military forces in the Netherlands -- filling the same role. In recent years many non-ordained individuals have received professional training in chaplaincy and are now appointed as chaplains in schools, hospitals, universities, prisons and elsewhere to work alongside or instead of ordained chaplains. (Norman, 2004)

Wikipedia states that although originally chaplain was a Christian term it is also now applied to people in other religions filling the same role. In recent years many non-ordained persons have received professional training in chaplaincy and are now appointed as chaplains in schools, hospitals, universities, prisons and elsewhere to work alongside or instead of ordained chaplains. (Wikipedia, 2003)

Although public awareness has increased in recent years, many, including the local church and the clergy do not understand the chaplain ministry, including the chaplain's role, relationship and challenges in the law enforcement community.   "The Law Enforcement Chaplains regularly visit the department for personal contact with law enforcement personnel and staff. They build trusting relationships and establish credibility. Riding with the officers on their shifts is vital to a successful ministry. Chaplains also provide guidance ad confidential counseling for personal, family, and job-related problems to both sworn and civilian personnel, their families and others. They refer those in need of professional help to qualified counselors. Chaplains assist families of officers/staff personnel/victims in times of serious injury, illness or death. They respond immediately to emergency situations involving departmental personnel and victims. Chaplains maintain an updated list of spiritual and social service providers, to whom they refer departmental personnel, victims and their families." (Wisegeek, 2003)

CHAPTER 2
AN EXPLORATION OF CHAPLAINCY
LITERATURE REVIEW
Sociological Challenges and Chaplain Ministry

Matthew chapter 25 concerns Jesus' teaching about the value of all persons—not just those who shared his ethnicity, culture, and religion. Jesus taught that if people wanted to be considered "righteous" and "inherit the kingdom" of God, they were to minister to all persons, particularly those considered the "least of these. (Paget & McCormack, 2006)

Many of the people who were considered the "least of these" are still with us. They are the homeless, the disabled, the uneducated, and the terminally ill. Chaplains are called to minister to the disenfranchised of society—the "least of these." (Paget & McCormack, 2006)

On the other hand, chaplains face the challenge of providing loving care to all they encounter—even those whose social or economic status doesn't seem to warrant help or those whose celebrity already commands attention or assistance. Other times the challenge is providing and demonstrating the love of God to those whom don't seem to deserve care—the perpetrator of heinous crimes or the one who threatens the Christian faith. (Paget & McCormack, 2006)

The Matthew text speaks to the chaplain of the innate worth of all persons, not just those who agree with their religion, share their culture, or look like them. Because we are all "created in the image of God" (Genesis 1:27), we are all entitled to, and worthy of, compassionate ministry and respect. No one is outside the love or concern of God (John 3:16). Chaplains follow God's example by loving and caring for each person. (Paget & McCormack, 2006)

Types of chaplains
Health care
Many hospitals and hospices employ chaplains to assist
with the spiritual needs of patients, families and staff. "The
Healthcare Chaplain, an integral member of the healthcare
team, makes daily rounds and is available 24-hours a day to
provide pastoral care for patients/residents, family and
staff. The Chaplain is available to provide objective crisis
intervention and competent spiritual support." (Wikipedia,
2003)

Wikipedia adds that in the United States, health care
chaplains are typically educated through the Association
for Clinical Pastoral Education and may be certified by one
of the following organizations: The Association of
Professional Chaplains, The National Association of
Catholic Chaplains, The National Association of Jewish
Chaplains, or The College of Pastoral Supervision and
Psychotherapy. Certification typically requires a Masters of
Divinity degree (or its equivalent), faith group ordination or
commissioning, faith group endorsement, and four units
(1600 hours) of Clinical Pastoral Education (the Military
Chaplains Association of the United States of America does
require more, but they are a dod2088 501c-3 military
support group founded in 1954 by Military Chaplains).
(United States Marine Chaplains Association.com, April
28, 2010)

In Canada, Health Care Chaplains may be certified by
the Canadian Association for Pastoral Practice and
Education. (Wikipedia, 2006)
In England, Health Care Chaplains are employed by their
local NHS Trust or by charities associated with hospice.
The majority work part-time, combining their role with
another post, either in a local Church or another chaplaincy.
The professional body in England is the College of Health
Care Chaplains. In Scotland and Northern Ireland, the
bodies are the Scottish Association of Chaplains in

Healthcare (SACH) and the Northern Ireland Healthcare Chaplains Association. Membership of the College of Health Care Chaplains is not compulsory but may be advantageous as it carries with it membership of a Trade Union. Chaplains working in a palliative care setting may also choose to join the Association of Hospice and Palliative Care Chaplains. (Wikipedia, 2009)

Military

"A chaplain provides spiritual and pastoral support for service personnel, including the conduct of religious services at sea or in the field. Military chaplains have a long history; the first English military-oriented chaplains, for instance, were priests on board proto-naval vessels during the eighth century A.D. Land based chaplains appeared during the reign of King Edward I. The current form of military chaplain dates from the era of the First World War." (Willmott, 2003)

Wikipedia goes on to convey that chaplains are nominated, appointed, or commissioned in different ways in different countries. A military chaplain can be an army-trained soldier with additional theological training or a priest nominated to the army by religious authorities. In the United Kingdom the Ministry of Defence employs chaplains but their authority comes from their sending church. Royal Navy chaplains undertake a 16 week bespoke induction and training course including a short course at Britannia Royal Naval College and specialist fleet time at sea alongside a more experienced chaplain. Naval Chaplains called to service with the Royal Marines undertake a grueling 5 month long Commando Course, and if successful wear the commandos' Green Beret. British Army chaplains undertake seven weeks training at The Armed Forces Chaplaincy Centre Amport House and The Royal Military Academy Sandhurst. Royal Air Force chaplains must complete 12 weeks Specialist Entrant course at the RAF College Cranwell followed by a Chaplains' Induction Course at Armed Forces Chaplaincy Centre Amport House of a further 2 weeks. In the United States military, chaplains must be endorsed by their religious affiliation in order to serve in any facet of the military. (Army Chaplain Corps; Air Force Chaplain Agency, April 28, 2010)

Military Chaplains are normally accorded officer status, although Sierra Leone had a Naval Lance Corporal chaplain in 2001. In most navies, their badges and insignia do not differentiate their levels of responsibility and status. By contrast, in Air Forces and Armies, they typically carry ranks and are differentiated by crosses or other equivalent religious insignia. According to official website of the Air Force Chaplain Corps, "Air Force people live and work around the world serving our country. Chaplains serve side-by-side with them, leading worship services and observances, providing pastoral care, and advising leadership as they magnify the Air Force Chaplain Corps vision of Glorifying God, Serving Airmen, and Pursuing Excellence." However, United States military chaplains Association and every branch carry both rank and Chaplain Corps insignia. (Wikipedia, 2008)

"Though the Geneva Conventions do not state whether chaplains may bear arms, they specify (Protocol I, 8 June 1977, Art 43.2) that chaplains are noncombatants. In recent years both the UK and U.S. have required chaplains, but not medical personnel, to be unarmed. Other nations, notably Norway, Denmark and Sweden, make it an issue of individual conscience. Captured chaplains are not considered Prisoners of War (Third Convention, 12 August 1949, Chapter IV Art 33) and must be returned to their home nation unless retained to minister to prisoners of war." (Wikipedia, 2009)

Inevitably, a significant number of serving chaplains have died in action. The U.S. Army and Marines lost 100 chaplains killed in action during WWII: a casualty rate greater "than any other branch of the services except the infantry and the Army Air Corps" (Crosby, 1994, pxxiii). Many have been decorated for bravery in action (five have won Britain's highest award for gallantry, the <u>Victoria Cross</u>). The <u>Chaplain's Medal for Heroism</u> is a special <u>U.S. military decoration</u> given to military chaplains who have been killed in the line of duty, although it has to date only been awarded to the famous <u>Four Chaplains</u>, all of whom died in the <u>USAT *Dorchester*</u> sinking in 1943 after giving up their lifejackets to others. (Wikipedia, 2003)

The <u>United States European Command</u> has co-sponsored an annual *<u>International Military Chiefs of Chaplains Conference</u>* every year since 1991. (Wikipedia, 2003)

At times, the existence of military chaplains has been challenged in countries that have a <u>separation of Church and State</u>. (Hitchens & Sharpton, 2007)

According to America's Navy website article *"What Will You Do?"* the Navy Chaplains serve on ships and at foreign and domestic bases throughout various Navies, Marine Corps and Coast Guard commands. Responsibilities associated with Navy Chaplain jobs may include:

Conduct worship services in a variety of settings

Perform religious rites and ceremonies such as weddings and funeral services

Counsel individuals who seek guidance

Oversee religious education programs, such as Sunday school and youth groups

Visit and provide spiritual guidance and care to hospitalized personnel and/or their family members

Train lay leaders who conduct religious education programs

Promote attendance at religious services, retreats, and conferences

Parliamentary

Some nations, including the United States, have chaplains appointed to work with parliamentary bodies, such as the Chaplain of the United States Senate, and the Chaplain of the United States House of Representatives. In addition to opening proceedings with prayer, these chaplains provide pastoral counseling to congressional members, their staffs, and their families; coordinate the scheduling of guest chaplains, who offer opening prayers; arrange and sometimes conduct marriages, memorial services, and funeral services for congress, staff, and their families; and conduct or coordinate religious services, study groups, prayer meetings, holiday programs, and religious education programs, as well. (Wikipedia, 2003)

Law Enforcement

Law Enforcement Chaplains serve in local, county, state and federal agencies and provide a variety of important services within the law enforcement community. (Chaplain Fellowship Ministries) They should not be confused with Prison Chaplains, whose primary ministry is to those who are incarcerated either awaiting trial or after conviction. The role of the Law Enforcement Chaplain deals primarily with Law Enforcement personnel and agencies. Law enforcement officers are faced with having to make split second decisions which at times cause a tremendous amount of anxiety, frustration and criticism for doing their jobs. Many times this will create problems for the officers and their families as well as often being reflected in their job performance and, or, their on the job attitudes towards both others officers and the public that they serve. The chaplain responds to these unique needs and challenges with spiritual guidance, reassuring and trustworthy presence, resources and counseling services. Also, Law Enforcement chaplains are often involved as resource providers in assisting with hostage negotiations, death notifications in the community, public relations and other needs that the law enforcement agency might have. (Chaplain Fellowship Ministries, April 28, 2010) Law Enforcement Chaplains regularly visit the department for personal contact with law enforcement personnel and staff. They build trusting relationships and establish credibility. Riding with the officers on their shifts is vital to a successful ministry. (Chaplain Fellowship Ministries) Chaplains also provide guidance and confidential counseling for personal, family, and job-related problems to both sworn and civilian personnel, their families and others. They refer those in need of professional help to qualified counselors. Chaplains assist families of officers/staff personnel/victims in times of serious injury, illness or death. They respond immediately to emergency situations involving departmental personnel and victims. Chaplains maintain an updated list of spiritual and social service providers, to whom they refer departmental personnel, victims, and their families. (Wikipedia, 2003)

Chaplains also conduct worship services and Scriptural Studies as needed. (Chaplain Fellowship Ministries) One aspect of the ministries of Law Enforcement chaplains, like other chaplains working in the public sector (such as those serving in the military) is the need for effective ecumenical outreach, accepting all personnel that they minister to where they are in their faith journey. (Chaplain Fellowship Ministries) Law Enforcement chaplains often have information about who can provide worship resources for other faiths, and also for the various denominations and groups within their own faith. (Chaplain Fellowship Ministries) They offer invocations and benedictions at academy graduations, award ceremonies, and civic and social events, as requested. (Wikipedia, 2001)

Often the Law Enforcement chaplain is the only minister with whom law enforcement can relate. Occasionally, the chaplain is asked to conduct, or participate in, weddings and funerals by the officers or their families. The chaplain responds to the need as an opportunity for ministry and witness. Chaplains participate in basic law enforcement training. They sometimes become training resource leaders themselves in their areas of expertise, particularly in the cultural and practical aspects of differing faith and ethnic communities within their agency's particular jurisdiction. Law enforcement officers often need someone whom they feel that they can trust to assist them with death notifications, suicide attempts, emotionally upset people who have been traumatized, and a myriad of other problems and challenges. They also need someone to care for their families and themselves during times of trauma or distress. (Chaplain Fellowship Ministries, April 28, 2010)

The Law Enforcement chaplain offers support to Law Enforcement Officers, Administrators, Support Staff, Victims and their families, and occasionally even the families of accused or convicted offenders. (Chaplain Fellowship Ministries) The role of the chaplain within Law Enforcement is an important one in American culture. (Wikipedia, 2003)

Fire Department

Chaplains working with fire departments provide the same kind of support to firefighters as do chaplains working with law enforcement, and sometimes face even greater danger, working with the wounded in often very dangerous surroundings. (Wikipedia, 2003)

At the scene of the September 11 attacks on New York's World Trade Center, for example, Franciscan Monk fire chaplain, Fr. Mychal F. Judge, lost his life when he re-entered one of the World Trade Center buildings, shortly after administering last rites to a wounded firefighter. (Wakin, 2002)

Corporate

Some businesses, large or small, employ chaplains for their staff and/or clientele. According to *The Economist* (August 25 2007, p64) there are 4,000 corporate chaplains in the U.S. alone, with the majority being employees of specialist chaplaincy companies such as Marketplace Chaplains USA or Corporate Chaplains of America. According to the Marketplace Chaplains USA, turnover at Taco Bell outlets in central Texas dropped by a third after they started employing chaplains. Workplace Chaplain Organizations, such as Marketplace Chaplains Europe and Capellania Empresarial in

Sports

A sports chaplain provides pastoral care for the sports person and the broader sports community including the coach, administrators and their families. (Wikipedia, 2003) Chaplains to sports communities have existed since the middle of the 20th century and have significantly grown in the past 20 years. The United States, United Kingdom and Australia have well established Christian sports chaplaincy ministries. (Wikipedia, 2003)

Sports Chaplains consist of people from many different walks of life. Most commonly, the chaplains are ministers or full time Christian workers but occasionally, chaplaincy work is done without charge or any financial remuneration. Often, sports chaplains to a particular sport are former participants of that sport. This helps the chaplain to not only provide spiritual support and guidance to a player, but gives them the ability to empathize and relate to some of the challenges facing the participant with whom they are ministering. (Wikipedia, 2003)

Domestic

A domestic chaplain was a chaplain attached to a noble household in order to grant the family a degree of self-sufficiency in religion. The chaplain was freed from any obligation to reside in a particular place so could travel with the family, internationally if necessary, and minister to their spiritual needs. Further, the family could appoint a chaplain who reflected their own doctrinal views. Domestic chaplains performed family christenings, funerals and weddings and were able to conduct services in the family's private chapel, excusing the nobility from attending public worship. (Gibson, 1997)

In feudal times most laymen, and for centuries even most noblemen, were poorly educated and the chaplain would also be an important source of scholarship in the household, tutoring children and providing counsel to the family on matters broader than religion. (Gibson, 1997) Before the advent of the legal profession, modern bureaucracy and civil service, the literate clergy were often employed as secretarial staff, as in a chancery. Hence the term *clerk*, derived from Latin *clericus* (clergyman). This made them very influential in temporal affairs. There was also a moral impact since they heard the confessions of the elite. (Wikipedia, 2003)

The domestic chaplain was an important part of the life of the peerage in England from the reign of Henry VIII to the middle of the nineteenth century. Up until 1840, Anglican domestic chaplains were regulated by law and enjoyed the substantial financial advantage of being able to purchase a license to hold two benefices simultaneously while residing in neither. (Gibson, 1997)

Many monarchies and major noble houses had, or still have, several domestic or private chaplains as part of their Ecclesiastical Household, either following them or attached to a castle or other residence. Queen Elizabeth II has 36 Anglican chaplains, in addition to chaplains extraordinary and honorary chaplains appointed to minister to her. Castles with attached chaplains generally had at least one Chapel Royal, sometimes as significant as a cathedral. A modern example is <u>St George's Chapel, Windsor Castle</u>, also the home of the <u>Order of the Garter</u>. (Wikipedia, 2003)

Educational Institutions

Chaplains are appointed by many educational institutions, including colleges and universities, sometimes working directly for the institution, and sometimes as representatives of separate organizations that specifically work to support students, such as Hillel College Campus Ministry for Jews, and Newman House, College Campus Ministry, for Catholics. <u>The National Association of College and University Chaplains</u> works to support the efforts of many of these chaplains, helping chaplains minister to the individual faith of students, faculty, and staff, while promoting interreligious understanding. Chaplains often also oversee programs on campus that foster spiritual, ethical, religious, and political and cultural exchange, and the promotion of service. (Wikipedia, 2003)

<u>Imam Yahya Hendi</u>, is Muslim Chaplain for Washington DC's Georgetown University, the first American university to hire a full-time Muslim chaplain. (Wikipedia, 2003)

"Reliable workplace statistics suggest that in an average year 17% of the workforce will experience a crisis event that will interrupt or adversely affect their work activity. Across the nation a growing number of agencies like ours are providing timely, cost effective, on-site and off-site care that gives such employees the best chance of managing such events in a positive and productive way." [http://www.workplacechaplains.us/, 1999]

Workplace Chaplains goes on to say that whether as a supplement to an existing EAP program or a stand-alone employee assistance option, this contracted service provides confidential, convenient, and professional counsel, comfort, and referral to employees and their families. (<u>http://workplacechaplains.us/</u>, 1999)

Other

Chaplains also can be attached to sports teams, emergency services agencies, private clubs, groups such as Boys and Girls Brigade companies and scout troops, ships, hospitals, prisons, nightclubs, private companies, theatres and corporations. Chaplains also serve in hospice programs and retirement centers. The term can also refer to priests attached to Roman Catholic convents. (Wikipedia, 2003)

CHAPTER 3
THE IMPORTANCE OF COUNSELING OTHERS

The Religious Ministry Team Handbook expresses that, "This is the act of a chaplain or member of the clergy providing theological, spiritual or religious direction, opinion, instruction and/or advice assisting a person in making moral/ethical choices affecting their conduct, judgment, and/or decisions. Commanders can expect chaplains to be qualified pastoral counselors in accordance with their theological training and professional education. (Marine Corps Reference Publication (MCRP) 5-1, 2003)

Pastor counseling is not psychological or clinical. Pastoral counsel is direction, instruction, advice or guidance, based on theological foundations or religious beliefs, provided by a member of the clergy or a professional minister, assisting a person in arriving at a moral/ethical judgment, decision or understanding. (MCRP 5-1, 2003)

Chaplains provide pastoral counseling for Marines, Sailors, and their family members for a variety of personal concerns including the following:
Personal faith and spiritual development.
Pre-marriage/marriage.
Career choices and life decisions.
Conflict resolution, grief and personal loss,
Anger and crisis intervention.
Suicide ideation and intervention
Conscientious objection and immunization waivers, etc.
Marines and Sailors often feel more comfortable speaking with their chaplain concerning personal issues or problems before approaching another health care professional.
(MCRP 5-1, 2003)

IMPORTANCE OF THE ROLE OF MILITARY CHAPLAINS AND OTHER CLERGY IN SERVING VICTIMS OF CRIME
Americans' primary source of help for problems
1960's Study
42% Clergy
29% General Physicians
17% Psychiatrists
10% Other Mental Health Professionals
2% Other
25 years later (after Community Mental Health)
34% Clergy
28% Community Health Centers
Lesser percentages in each of all other disciplines.
Percentages do not necessarily apply to chaplains. From all indicators, and depending upon the particular command, it is estimated that well over 50% of military personnel see chaplains as primary source of help.

DEFINITIONS

Physical Abuse
Physical abuse is that treatment of a child which results in injuries caused by hitting, pushing, whipping, biting, punching, slapping, or burning. Injuries include bruises, burns, welts, cuts and bone and skull fractures.

Sexual Abuse
Sexual abuse is any person, adult or child, forcing, tricking, threatening or coercing a child to have <u>any</u> kind of sexual contact with her or him. It may range from intercourse by rape or incest to touching inappropriately and exposure.

Emotional Abuse
Emotional abuse is excessive verbal assault (belittling, screaming, threatening, blaming, using sarcasm), unpredictable responses (inconsistency), continual negative moods, constant family discord and double-message

communication.
Physical Neglect
Physical neglect is failure to provide a child with adequate food, shelter, clothing, protection, supervision and medical and dental care.

CHILD NEGLECT
Most Frequently Reported
Character Disorders of Neglectful Parents
Apathy - Futility Syndrome
Impulse Ridden
Many Children - One Dysfunctional Parent
The other "takes up slack"
Neglected Child -- Both Parents or his/her only parent are Dysfunctional or He/She Has Parent Exhibiting Neglectful Parent Characteristics

---

NEGLECTFUL PARENTS

Less
Involved with others
Able to plan
Able to control impulses
Confident regarding the future
Verbally accessible
More
Psychological psychosomatic symptoms
Socially isolated
Isolated from helping networks
(Informal/formal)

INDICATORS OF POSSIBLE CHILD NEGLECT
Child's Appearance
Consistently dirty, unwashed, hungry, or inappropriately dressed

Without supervision for extended periods of time or when engaged in dangerous activities

Constantly tired or listless

Has unattended physical problems or lacks routine medical care

Is exploited, overworked, or kept from attending school

Has been abandoned

NEGLECT INDICATORS
Child's Behavior
Is engaging in delinquent acts (e.g., vandalism, drinking, prostitution, drug use, etc.)

Is begging or stealing food

Rarely attends school

Caretaker's Behavior
Misuses alcohol or other drugs

Maintains chaotic home life

Shows evidence of apathy or futility

Is mentally ill or of diminished intelligence

Has history of neglect as a child

CHILD PHYSICAL ABUSE
Usually related to "discipline" (trying to enforce behavior)

Generally inflicted when caretaker is out of control

Often caused by failure to understand stages of child development (expectations beyond child's capability)

More frequent when caretaker's primary method of training is physical coercion

More likely when control takes precedence over nurture

INDICATORS OF POSSIBLE PHYSICAL CHILD ABUSE
Child's Appearance
Bruises or welts on body or face

Burns (particularly a burn that shows the shape of the item used, such as an iron, stove burner or cigarette)

Fractures

Lacerations and abrasions (especially around the mouth, lip, eye, or external genitalia).

Human bite marks

Child's Behavior

Wary of physical contact with adults

Demonstrates extremes in behavior (either extreme aggressiveness or withdrawal)

Seems afraid of parents

Reports injury by parents

PHYSICAL ABUSE INDICATORS
Caretaker's Behavior

Has history of abuse as a child

Uses harsh discipline inappropriate to child's age, transgression, and condition

Has performance expectations which are beyond the age capabilities of the child

Offers illogical, unconvincing, contradictory, or no explanation of child's injury

Seems unconcerned about child

Significantly misperceives child (e.g., sees child as bad, evil, a monster, etc.)

Psychotic or psychopathic

Misuses alcohol or other drugs

Attempts to conceal child's injury or to protect identity of person responsible

CHILD SEXUAL ABUSE
Myths

1. Sexual abuse of children is rather rare
2. Most molesters are "dirty old men"
3. Most child sexual abuse is by strangers
4. Primarily in rural and lower socio-economic backgrounds
5. Not likely in religious families

6. Should not talk with child about it for fear of frightening

7. Most takes place in isolated, deserted areas

8. Adolescents should be held accountable for encountering sexual assault

---

INDICATORS OF POSSIBLE CHILD SEXUAL ABUSE

Child's Appearance

Has torn, stained, or bloody underclothing

Experiences pain or itching in the genital area

Has bruises or bleeding in external genitalia, vagina, or anal regions

Has venereal disease

Has swollen or red cervix, vulva, or perineum

Has semen around mouth or genitalia or on clothing

Is pregnant

Child's Behavior

Appears withdrawn or engaged in fantasy or infantile behavior

Has poor peer relationships

Is unwilling to participate in physical activities

Is engaging in delinquent acts or runs away

States he/she has been sexually assaulted by parent/caretaker

Caretaker's Behavior

Extremely protective or jealous of child

Encourages child to engage in prostitution or sexual acts in the presence of caretaker

Has been sexually abused as a child

Is experiencing marital difficulties

Misuses alcohol or other drugs

Is frequently absent from home

RESPONSE TO DISCLOSURE OF CHILD SEXUAL ABUSE

1. Listen to the child and take seriously what she/he says.
2. Stay calm.
3. Thank the child and reassure that it is not her/his fault.
4. Take immediate steps to protect the child.
5. Report the suspected abuse immediately.
6. Continue to give support as the child goes through the child protection system.
7. Have the child seen by a physician.
8. Find a professional in the field or a colleague to talk to. This person should definitely commit to holding confidentiality.
9. Find out if the court is going to recommend treatment for the child. Make contact with the therapist and offer to cooperate.
10. Continue to offer the child the emotional support she/he needs.
11. Take steps to assure that the sexual abuse does not happen again.

CHILD EMOTIONAL ABUSE - DEFINITION AND DYNAMICS
<u>EMOTIONAL ABUSE</u>
Verbal or emotional assault
Close confinement
Threatened harm
<u>EMOTIONAL NEGLECT</u>
Inadequate nurturance/affection
Knowingly permitting maladaptive behavior (Example - delinquency)
Refusal to provide essential care
PRESENT IN OTHER FORMS OF CHILD ABUSE AND NEGLECT
<u>COMPONENTS</u>

Rejecting
Isolating
Terrorizing
Ignoring
Corrupting

CONTINUUM OF PARENTAL BEHAVIOR

POSITIVE PARENTAL BEHAVIOR:	NEGATIVE PARENTAL BEHAVIOR:	EMOTIONAL MALTREATMENT:
Praising Attention Affection Good Example Guidance	Yelling Name Calling Ignoring Over Prohibition Over Control	Consistent Negative Behaviors Rejecting Threatening Bizarre Punishment Using

INDICATORS OF POSSIBLE EMOTIONAL MALTREATMENT

Child's Appearance
Emotional maltreatment, often less tangible than other forms of child abuse and neglect, can be indicated by behaviors of the child and the caretaker.
Child's Behavior
Appears overly compliant, passive, undemanding
Is extremely aggressive, demanding or enraged
Shows overly adaptive behaviors, either inappropriately adult or inappropriately infantile
Rocks, sucks thumb, is enuretic
Lags in physical, emotional, and intellectual development
Attempts suicide
Caretaker's Behavior
Blames or belittles child

Is cold and rejecting
Withholds love
Treats siblings unequally
Seems unconcerned about child's problems

MANDATE TO REPORT
All states now have a mandated Child Abuse Reporting
Law
Military requires reporting to Family Advocacy
The list of Mandated Reporters generally includes:

Law Enforcement Personnel
Medical Practitioners
Day Care Operators
Teachers (Public and Private Schools)
Therapists and Counselors
School Administrators
Group Home Personnel
Social Workers
Photo Processing Stores & Labs

In some states clergy are also mandated.
In most, as well as in the military, exceptions are made
because of privilege of confidentiality.

However, if clergy person also falls under one of the above
categories, he/she is mandated.

There is, however, a moral obligation to report in order to
protect the child.

PRIVILEGE OF CONFIDENTIALITY
VS
IMPERATIVE TO REPORT

The conflict: Protecting Children (intervention in abuse) vs.

Maintaining Confidence
If indicators are observed (vs. Being revealed in pastoral consultation) no violation of confidence in reporting
Question: What to do when revealed in confidential pastoral counseling setting?
Conflict of Ethics:
Ethics of maintaining confidence vs. Ethic of reporting to protect the child
Scriptures place high emphasis upon the welfare of child (Matthew 18:2-6)

CONFIDENTIALITY (Continued)
Range of Religious Positions on Confidentiality
Roman Catholic, Episcopal, & Eastern Orthodox --
Confessional churches
Excommunicated if information told in confession is
revealed
Many Protestant & Free Churches "Maintain all
confidences"
Jewish -- Not a confessional faith
Disclosure for safety of victim important
Evangelical Lutheran Church in America (ELCA) "No
disclosure without permission,
or if the person is perceived to intend great harm to self and
others"
Note: Other denominations are now establishing similar
directives in their pastoral conduct procedures.
Difference between secrecy and confidentiality
Secrecy -- Never disclose
Confidentiality -- A trust shared only with
permission or in the interest of person involved. (Note:
New transparency T-60 follows this transparency.)

MYTHS (M) AND FACTS (F)
ABOUT DOMESTIC VIOLENCE

M Only in small percentage of population

F 28% of all marriages
90% go unreported

M Not as frequent in middle or upper class homes

F - Every race, religion, socio-economic background, and
profession

- More "poor" battered women in shelters because of lack of resources
- Wealthier victims -- more to lose if they report

M Alcohol abuse causes violence

F 40 - 80% of the time alcohol is a factor
Alcohol does not cause abuse -- lowers inhibitions so that abuser's nature more easily expressed.

M Abusers are "Psychopathic", "Sick", "Evil"

F May lead "normal" lives in all aspects except inability to control aggressive impulses
Result of poor self-image
Need to live up to society's image of masculinity
Often charming and manipulative (either "very good" or "very bad")

M Victims are masochistic, provoke assaults, enjoy violence

F Male partners provoke violence 85% of time
Examples: Baby crying
Dinner not ready on time, etc.
Extent of violence - which escalates:
Hitting in face
Kicking in abdomen
Throwing against wall
Bones broken
Eyes swollen
Lips lacerated

M Some women deserve beating to keep them in line

Historically men had both right and obligation to keep their "children, cattle and wives from transgressing"
Women are not property
No one has right to control another by violence

M Strong faith will prevent battering

F Depends on nature of "faith"
Sometimes religion has been used to condone wife beating

M Shelters break up families

F Hospitals don't cause accidents. Violence breaks up families

---

A CYCLE OF VIOLENCE
Phase I
Tension
Building

Phase II
Explosion
Incident

Phase III
Regret/Hearts & Flowers

BATTERED WOMEN STAY BECAUSE
Their childhood experience in controlled, authoritarian home
They still love their husband -- hope they can change him
They believe it is their responsibility to insure peace and success of the family
They are socially and economically dependent on abusing partner

They believe a violent father is better than no father at all
Of scriptural injunctions against separation and divorce
Of pastoral counsel that the family stay together at all costs
QUESTION:
Is a violent dysfunctional family wherein children are
terrorized and emotionally traumatized a scriptural family?

AN OVERVIEW OF CHILDREN WHO WITNESS DOMESTIC VIOLENCE

Children often appear:
Sad, fearful, depressed and/or anxious
Aggressively defiant or passively compliant
To have limited tolerance for frustration and stress
To become isolated and withdrawn
To be at risk for drug and alcohol abuse, sexual acting out, running away
To have poor impulse control
To feel powerless
To have low self esteem
To take on parental roles

DOMESTIC VIOLENCE

Guidelines for Clergy
1. It occurs in most, if not all, congregations
2. Victims often try to conceal battery
3. Domestic violence is a crime -- cannot be tolerated
4. Requires specialized therapy
5. Ask the question -- usually not volunteered
6. Victims may open up with hints and indirection
7. Victims test to determine reaction
8. Listen to the victim -- affirm feeling
9. Challenge violence
10. Make certain that faith statements do not perpetuate the violence

11. Assist in looking for empowering solutions
12. See victim's safety as a high priority
13. Offer options:
Individual counsel
Support groups
Career counsel
Social services
Shelter
Legal aid
Education
14. Let victim make the choices
15. Support victim's choices
16. Help victim discover resources:
Money - Friends - Relatives - Employment
17. Confront what is happening to children
18. Make it your goal to get victim in Domestic
Violence Program if possible
19. Continue support through the process
20. Assure confidentiality
21. Do not suggest marriage or couples counseling!
22. Give the victim time
23. Be prepared for frustration
24. Give Scriptural faith assurances - and encourage victim
to draw upon God's strength
25. Learn your community's resources:
Shelter programs
Batterer's programs
Self-help groups
AA
Therapists
Prosecutor's Office

DOMESTIC VIOLENCE CRISIS COUNSELING
Do not go to the home
Call police
Ask if violence is over and how victim is

Ask where children are
Ask if she fears abuser will come back
Does she have a safe place to go?
How will she get there?
Tell her of victim's programs (including battered women's shelter and victim/ witness assistance programs)
Give emotional support
Offer assistance with the process (with specialists)

CONGREGATIONAL ASSISTANCE
Post-emergency Hot Lines and Shelter numbers
Assist shelters with food, clothing -- volunteers
Assist both victim and perpetrator with basic needs
Assist with housing of a victim (only if recommended by shelter and treatment programs)
Congregational exchange of homes
Create a shelter
Sponsor forums on Domestic Violence
Subscribe to newsletters
Form a study group on religious issues

RAPE -- SEXUAL ASSAULT
Definition -- Forced penetration by the penis or any object into the vagina, mouth or anus against the will of the victim.
Improvement over previous definition which defined rape as vaginal intercourse forced by a male on a female.
The act involves sexual activity because of genital contact, but it is committed to primarily fulfill non-sexual needs
Power (control)
Anger (hostility)
Aggression (disposition to violence)
Rape can be committed in marital and dating relationships
Most frequently committed violent act

RAPE MYTHS
1. Rape is a crime of passion
It is a crime of power and control
2. Women who are careful don't get raped
High percentage (not majority) occur in home, workplace and school
3. Rape is impossible if the woman really resists
Rapists usually has advantage of surprise and strength
4. Women secretly want to be raped
Difference between romantic fantasy and violent reality -- no one wants loss of control
5. Rapist is usually a stranger
Yes, according to BJS, but other surveys, particularly on college campuses, 84% knew offender, 66% date rape
6. Women invite rape by seductive dress
Little correlation between attractiveness and likelihood of rape
7. If rape is imminent the woman should relax and enjoy it
Compliance or non-forceful resistance are not necessarily deterrents to murder
8. Women "Cry Rape"
Sexual assault one of most underreported crimes

IMPACT OF RAPE
Physical, Emotional, Psychological
Immediate
Fear, anger, outrage or
Controlled style of response
Initially
Sense of disorganization
Fear
Shame
Humiliation
Degradation
Guilt
Anger

Self-blame
Revenge
Mood swings
First few days or weeks
Acute physical symptoms
Soreness: stomach, arms, throat, legs
Muscle tension -- disturbance of sleep
Distressed, irritable, jumpy
Affected eating patterns
Long-term
Difficulty returning to daily schedule
Desire to change job/school/ residence
Sleeplessness -- Nightmares
Phobias
Sexual concerns
Trust issues
Social isolation

STAGES OF ADJUSTMENT TO RAPE -- SEXUAL ASSAULT
Shock "I'm numb"
Denial "This can't have happened"
Anger "What did I do? Why me?"
Bargaining "Let's go on as if it didn't happen"
Depression "I feel so dirty and worthless"
Acceptance "Life can go on"
Assimilation "It's part of my life"

SEXUAL ASSAULT AND THE LAW
Rape Shield Laws -- Past sexual relations inadmissible
Victim Resistance -- Changes in law make it unnecessary for victim to prove resistance
Redefinition of Rape -- Gender-neutral
Changes in Penalty Structure -- Less possible to plead to lesser charge to avoid sexual connotation

FACTORS HAVING A NEGATIVE IMPACT IN PREPARING FOR COURT

Pressure to drop charges

Pressure to go through with court

Delays

Monetary and time costs

- To family and friends

- To victim

Degradation

Interview

- Questions and style

- Advice and explanations

- Pressures to either strengthen story or reduce to lesser offense

ACQUAINTANCE (DATE) RAPE

In our culture, men are socialized to believe that women do not really mean what they say.

Many of both sexes feel that certain behavior ("leading the man on") allows men to force sex.

Man may feel that the woman really wants it, but has to say "no" to be virtuous. If he pushes her, they both will get what they want.

Peer pressure to have sex on a date. Encouragement to "score".

Woman may fear that the man finds her unattractive if he does not initiate sex.

Man may tell woman he won't go out with her again if she doesn't have sex.

UCLA Study of Male Teen Attitudes
When it is O.K. to force sex:
54% If she said yes at first then changed her mind
39% If he spent a lot of money on her
54% If she "led him on"
36% If he is so "turned on" he can't stop

CLERGY - CONGREGATIONAL RESPONSE -- RAPE

Remember, rape is an assault -- an issue of power and control more than sex

Don't view rape in terms of seductiveness -- provocativeness/promiscuity -- proper dress and conduct

Avoid tendency to blame the victim

Immediately obtain medical and legal assistance

Encourage prosecution

Support victim through this entire difficult process

Be prepared to deal with strong emotions -- the violation is intimate

Bring positive spiritual consolation to counter guilt -- the crime was not her fault

Assist with marriage and family issues. Use specialists

The key word "Non-Jud mentalism

GENERAL CHARACTERISTICS OF ABUSED AND NEGLECTED ELDERLY PERSONS

Usually live in family environment with an adult child or other family member who abuses them.

May live in a care home which is failing to comply with state standards.

Overwhelming majority of abuse victims suffer from one or more disabilities making them vulnerable and service-demanding.

Often in some discomfort and in need of constant attention and in-depth care.

May need special diet, special hygiene care and demonstration of affection and caring.

May have history of family violence, alcoholism, drug abuse or other stress.

Inflation may be a threat to fixed income.

Caretaker may have limited income and use elderly person's income improperly for personal use.

INDICATORS OF ELDER ABUSE & NEGLECT

Malnutrition

Dehydration

Frequent or multiple decubiti

Poor personal hygiene

Unclean clothes or bedding

Withholding drugs by caretaker

Untreated physical or mental health problems

Inadequate heating or cooling

Multiple injuries, burns or bruises

Vague explanation of denial of obvious injury

Exaggerated defensiveness exhibited by caretaker

Over hostility towards client exhibited by caretaker

Unwillingness to discuss problems in presence of caretaker

Fearful of caretaker, but anxious to please

Failure to meet basic subsistence needs despite adequate income

Reliance on client's income by care-taker for personal needs

Legal documents signed by caretaker when elderly person is capable or forced power of attorney

ELDER ABUSE
The role of pastors and congregations in prevention and protection
Reporting
Visitation
Escort and Transportation
Property Services
Financial Services
Support After the Abuse
Spiritual Counsel

DEFINITIONS
Robbery -- The unlawful taking or attempt to take property that is in the immediate possession of another by force or threat of force.

Simple Assault -- Unlawful intentional inflicting, or attempted inflicting, or injury upon the person of another without use of a dangerous or deadly weapon.

Aggravated Assault -- Infliction or attempt to inflict serious bodily injury by means of a dangerous deadly weapon.

Burglary -- Unlawful entry of any fixed structure, vehicle, or vessel used for regular residence, industry or business, with or without force with the intent to commit larceny/theft.

Larceny-Theft -- Unlawful taking or attempted taking of property other than a motor vehicle (motor vehicle theft is a separate category) from another by stealth, without force and without deceit.

IMPACT OF BURGLARY ON VICTIM
Frustration because the crime is a low priority on police response.
Victim's strong desire to catch offender, does not seem to be as strong a desire on the part of law enforcement.
Insurance difficulties
Police report
Bids for replacement
Conflict over value of items
Delays
Loss of items of limited monetary value but great emotional value (treasured pictures & mementos -- irreplaceable).
Fear of repetition --
Loss of trust in others -- more suspicious
No legal resolution --

IMPACT OF AGGRAVATED ROBBERY ON VICTIMS
Loss of property
Injury
Shock -- Symptoms of post-traumatic stress disorder
Ripple effects of the crime on family & friends
Inconveniences caused by law enforcement and court process
Sometimes lack of access to specialized services
Spiritual challenges -- Lacks trust of others
What about forgiveness?
Children's relationship to peers & society

CLERGY AND CONGREGATIONAL RESPONSE TO NEEDS OF VICTIMS OF ROBBERY, ASSAULT AND BURGLARY
Do not under estimate trauma
Be aware of priceless nature of some apparently

inexpensive items -- mementos, etc.
Address the sense of disorder and violation
Theologically -- God does not always protect from
victimization, but is present in the pain to enable healing.
Help with insurance if the victim desires, but do not take
the attitude that insurance makes it right.
In extreme trauma (often caused by aggravated offenses)
refer to psychological counsel and/or support group.
Assist with victim compensation through local
victim/witness program
Use congregational resources to repair locks, put in
lighting, cover immediate expenses if loss of money, etc.

HOMICIDE (MURDER) - VEHICULAR HOMICIDE
Definition

Reckless or intentional taking of a human life by another

Comments
Nothing in life prepares one emotionally for this.
There is expectation of death at the end of a long life
Little or no expectation of death for youth or those in prime
of life (except in cases of terminal illness -- then there is
preparation time).

This Kind of Death
Is sudden - stunning - overwhelming
Has a dimension of cruelty or recklessness which
compounds the sorrow
Causes an acute sense of injustice - intensified by slowness
and complexity of court process
Is irrational

VIOLENT ASSAULT
(Particularly Homicide)
Normal stages of grief (per Kubler Ross) do not necessarily
apply

Shock and suddenness cause reactions more like PTSD
(even certain survival chemical changes)

Ministry needs to be to whatever emotion arises at the time,
which may not necessarily be in the normal stages of
denial, anger, powerlessness, depression and acceptance

Horror about suffering of victim

Preoccupation with survivors' personal loss

Attacks of panic

Faith Doubts:

"Why did God allow this to happen?"

"I want revenge, but I know that is not right."

"Where is the victim now?"

GRIEF
TRAUMA PRE-EXISTING
SPECIFIC CONDITIONS
PTSD
SYMPTOMS
REACTIONS TO DEATH
Denial - Anger - Powerlessness - Depression -
Acceptance

REACTIONS TO VIOLENT DEATH

Turmoil and numbness -- Shock and confusion both mental
and physical

Inability to accept news or comprehend it

Preoccupation with survivor's personal loss

Horror about suffering of the victim

Need to know every detail

Attacks of panic

Fixation on maintaining day-to-day routine -- sometimes shattered by outbursts of intense emotion

Restlessness and insomnia

Inability to concentrate

Flashbacks to death notification or imagined pictures of the event

Fear for one's own life or lives of loved ones

Self-blame for what survivor did to cause the event or did not do to prevent it

Hostility to everyone who cannot bring victim back to life

Utter hopelessness and helplessness

STRESS FACTORS
Method of death notification

Impact on other life changes

Unwanted and untimely demands

Necessary role changes

Financial stress

Misguided compassion
(*From NOVA Training)

"It's God's will"

"Your loved one is better off -- in heaven"

"God called him/her"

"You need to forgive the murderer"

"Pray for his redemption"

Responses from families and friends

"Get on with your life"

"Forget about the past"

"Concentrate on the ones you have left"

UNIQUE STRESSOR -- CRIMINAL JUSTICE SYSTEM

Survivors want justice and a return to order.
Become angry with anything less.

Some in justice system see this as wanting revenge.

Survivor perceives failure of system if arrest or prosecution or penalty is slow in coming.

Delays

Barring from court procedures

Failure to inform

Hope for a plea bargain if there are evidentiary problems

Disillusionment with plea bargain

<u>Problems with verdict</u>

<u>Problems with inappropriate sentence</u>

<u>Problems with appropriate sentence</u>

<u>Victim impact statement</u>

HOW TO BE OF COMFORT

Don't desert

Don't try to fix the pain

Listen with your heart

Accept all expressions of grief without censoring

Permit the bereaved opportunity to talk openly about the departed loved one

Remain available

Be sincere

FORGIVENESS

Timing is all important

Only when the victim will benefit

Only when the victim is ready

Affirm the victim. He or she may want to forgive, but can't

Assure that forgiveness is not forgetting

WHAT VICTIMS WANT TO SAY TO CLERGY

Don't explain

Don't take away my reality

Stay close

Remember me . . . for a long time

Don't be frightened of my anger

Listen to my doubt

Be patient

Help me deal with forgiveness with integrity

WHEN PERMISSION TO REPORT CANNOT BE OBTAINED FROM COUNSELEE

Clergy person's ability to motivate individual to self-report is vital
Therapeutic value of leading parishioner to self-report
Call forth awareness of personal sin if the one who divulges is the offended
Therapeutic use of "penance" and how it can motivate self-reporting (Reporting can even be a form of "penance.")
Is guilt a good thing for motivation of change?
Can the tool of discipleship be used?
Clergy person could articulate the principle of "conscience."
This document was last updated on March 19, 2007
(*Crime in the United States*, 2006)

Posttraumatic Stress Disorder is a fancy term for a condition we've been aware of for many years. More than three thousand years ago an affliction resembling PTSD was observed in soldiers who fought in the Trojan War. In the American Civil War, Union soldiers, in shock from killing and burying other young Americans, were diagnosed with "nostalgia." (Kates, 2008)

In World War I, it was called "soldier's heart," "effort syndrome," "trench neurosis," or "shellshock." Over 250,000 British troops alone are known to have developed shellshock. In World War II, shellshock became "combat fatigue." (Kates, 2008)

From the Vietnam War evolved its present label—PTSD. From the first war with Iraq, veterans' officials suspect Persian Gulf War Syndrome contract by American soldiers could be a form of PTSD. In all wars, the common factors are exposure to extreme violence and PTSD's ability to overwhelm and disable its victims. (Kates, 2008)

Initially, psychologists thought only combat soldiers became overwhelmed by horrible incidents. For instance more than sixty years after World War II, veterans who saw combat are still coming forward with PTSD. Professionals realized soon, however, that anybody exposed even once to grave injury, illness, crime or death could be shocked into a psychological stupor from which some never recover. (Kates, 2008)

Kates (2008) goes on to cite Murders, rapes, assaults... In the United States, more than 17,000 people are murdered each year, and their families are psychologically shattered by the brutal acts. Every year, almost 300,000 women, children, adolescents and men are raped, and some never heal. Many female illegal aliens develop PTSD after experiencing rape or robbery during their fearful run over the border. After tennis star Monica Seles was stabbed by a deranged fan, she recovered quickly from her injuries, but became a recluse for over two years while undergoing treatment for PTSD. The loss and carnage were so great in the Oklahoma City bombing, that survivors, witnesses and psychologist were treated for extreme posttraumatic stress. (Kates, 2008)

Although it is generally accepted that 1 percent of the population has PTSD at any one time, the American Psychiatric Association estimates that at some time in our lives, as many as 14 percent of us may develop PTSD. For people who are "at-risk," like combat veterans and victims of crime, the prevalence of PTSD shoots up to as high as 58 percent. With such high numbers, we will likely come into contact with someone who has PTSD. We could develop it ourselves. (Kates, 2008)

What to do about Cop Shock? Kates (2008) cites the key ingredient for ending the reactions is communication. Talking, not only to fellow officers but to other support sources.

Suppressed feelings have a way of exploding months or years after horrifying incidents, but facing these emotions immediately may prevent that from happening. It may also stop PtSD from developing later. (Kates, 2008)

By establishing a support system before a critical incident occurs, peace officers empower themselves. Preparing for the inevitable puts officers in control during a period when control is sometimes taken away. (Kates, 2008)

A support system is a network of people whom officers in crisis can turn to. It's a game plan for reducing stress.

Fellow officers
Family members
Civilian friends
Peer counselors and therapists
Clergy
Support groups

A support system also features a stress management plan. A plan may include routines such as exercise and relaxation procedures like deep breathing and yoga. If officers use these resources regularly, suddenly employing them will not be a hardship when circumstances are already distressing. (Kates, 2008)

With these staggering statistics we see the need for counseling others. Plus, we see the importance of the role of chaplain and other clergy in servicing victims of crime and the general population.

Benimoff's spiritual crisis heightened upon his return home to Fort Carson, Colorado. He withdrew emotionally from his wife and sons, creating tensions that threatened to shatter the family. He was assigned to work at Walter Reed Army Medical Center, where he counseled returning soldiers suffering from post-traumatic stress disorder—until he was diagnosed himself with PTSD. Finding himself in the role of patient rather than caregiver, connecting as an equal with his fellow sufferers, and revisiting scriptural readings that once again rang with meaning and truth, he began his most decisive battle: for the love of his family and for the chance to once again open his heart to the healing grace of God. (Benimoff, 2009)

CHAPTER 4
WORDS OF ASSURANCE

The following is a list of questions asked potential candidates for chaplaincy compiled by the America's Navy - U.S. Government website operated by the United States Navy Recruiting Command (1998) which I retrieved March 17, 2010 from http://www.navy.com/careers/officer/chaplain/. These questions are pertinent to my study. They, also, were instrumental in determining the questions I would pose to potential interviewees.

Sample Questions to Ask a Potential Chaplain:

What is it that interests you about being a Chaplain?
Have you ever served as a chaplain before?
What is your understanding of what a Chaplain does?
What previous experience(s) has/have helped prepare you to be a Chaplain?
Have you gone through any type of training to be a Chaplain?
If so, what, when, where?
What are three or four strengths of yours that will help you be an effective Chaplain?
What areas do you need to become stronger in to increase your effectiveness as a Chaplain?
Do you have experience speaking to small groups?
Do you have experience leading Bible study?
On a scale of 1-10, with 10 being the strongest, how skilled are you in developing relationships with individuals and families?

Attempts were made to base questions on the protocol prescribed in my thesis when interviewing the Newton Street police department staff. The proceeding questions were chosen to pose to a senior naval chaplain I was introduced to who, also, participates in security work and understands the role of chaplaincy within the confines of law enforcement.

Actual Questions Asked:
What do think of the chaplains' role in your department?
What about the chaplains you have in your department?
When it comes to the tragic things of the community; how can we [community, clergy, etc.] be a help in that way?
What life events led you to become a chaplain?
Did you attend a house of worship throughout your childhood?
What part of your job do you struggle with emotionally?
What part of your job brings you the most joy?
What makes you cry?
What frustrates and/or angers you?
What kind of education and training do you have that enables you to perform in this capacity?
What would you say to others considering Chaplaincy as a profession?
What is the role of a chaplain apart from the armed forces or institution and what is that chaplain's role between communities and police department?
Role of the Interviewer is to ask the questions, listen, and interject where necessary to keep the interviewee on task/topic. These interviews are recorded and then transcribed making necessary grammatical changes based upon the information gathered from the interviewee without losing its validity.
The protection methods utilized, if requested, are to protect the identity of the interviewee by using the initials of that individual without revealing their name. All of the information will be maintained in the confines of this document and reviewed only by the Long Beach Bible College Thesis Committee.

CHAPLAINS CONTRIBUTIONS:
1ST INTERVIEW WITH LAW ENFORCEMENT

Richard McCready [RM] sitting here today with an Interview with Sergeant Curtis [SC], the sergeant of Newton Street Division:

RM: What do think of the chaplains' role here in the department?

SC: The role of the chaplains within the department it's invaluable. It has provided … it is a conduit; a conduit between the Police Department and the community. It's a collaborated effort that has worked for both us as police officers are able to reach out to our chaplains who have contact with all segments of the community. And what we find is a lot of folks well they go to work every day; and they have time, well they find time to go to church and church is where they get there community information. The clergy within the Newton area and to the city are that conduit that are able to come meet with the police officers, listen to what's going on from the police officers perspective and then they act as they act as the folks that are putting the information out … They don't come to the police department and say this persons doing that wrong or that persons doing that wrong; no it's an information that's being shared both ways; the police department is saying, these are some of what the crime scenes are saying; These are some of the things we are looking at … The clergy is able to go back to their churches and they convey, here's how you make your community safer. Here are some of the concerns of the police department and the collaborated effort is invaluable. What police officers look to when they see and work with the clergy in the department and the Newton area is someone who has a shared interest as is keeping the community safe. It's been a good collaborated effort. It's probably one of the things that should've been done 30 years ago when the department when community policing became the forefront for solving crime the first persons they should have reached out to is the local clergy, invite them in and be forthcoming in sharing information and in return get the public more inviting to the police.

RM: What about the chaplains you have here?

SC: The chaplains that we have come to Newton they're unique. They have knowledge of this community. They have a shared interest and they are great guys. They've been friends of mine for some time, but if you remove the friend aspect it's been a working relationship that in times of crisis you reach out to the clergy, the chaplains that come here in times of celebration on community events we reach to them for help. To look to them for guidance and for community support. The two chaplains that come here they have Newton as their, it's their priority. It's something they look forward to. The officers at Newton look forward to have the clergies come; earlier here say a week unless called at a different time, but it's something that they've come to look forward to. It's been a great working tool as being the Community Services Work Supervisor; the bridge that's its help build with the community is invaluable. These relationships go back for many decades. Um, it's opened doors for me, within this division because the two chaplains that come here are very trusting, the community trusts them, we trust them, the police department trusts them. So it's a good working relationship. And, it's made me a better police officer and it would be the one recommendation I would pass onto all the supervisors or the police officers of the department should get to know the local chaplain. And, if they can immolate what Newton has they're going to be steps ahead.

RM: Thank you, sergeant for your wonderful remarks. Let me ask you another question. When it comes to the tragic things of the community; how can we be a help in that way?

SC: Well, if there's a tragedy or a news release or event that comes to the forefront of the community and the police are addressing it; what the clergy are able to do; they're able to get into the crowd or get the pulse, the heartbeat of the community and they are able to help the police understand what the concerns are of the community. What did the community see? Do they see the police as distrustful? Are they seeing the police as helpful? The community, this community is no different than any other community in America. They just want to be safe, they want to go to work, come home and enjoy their family. This clergy, these chaplains and chaplains throughout the department are able to be in essence the eyes and ears of the community relations officers. They're actually within the community; most live within that community and when something happens they're the first people that we call to say, Hey, this is what happened; these are the actions the police department took and these are the reasons ... what are you hearing? Is it something different? And, if it is different it allows the police department to make adjustments to say if the message isn't getting out clearly or if the perception is wrong then the clergy is able to bring it to the forefront. It works great! It's been good

2ND INTERVIEW WITH MILITARY CHAPLAIN

Although the interviewee did not request amenity the following interview will be conducted simply as a Q & A interview.

Question: What do think of the chaplains' role in your department?

Answer: The role of chaplain ... I operate on a personal level, of course, being filled with the Holy Ghost. I, also, operate on the set premise for NAVS for Naval Chaplains which states if there is a religion that has been approved in the Hall of Congress then it is my duty to be able to minister and administer anything that relates to that particular religion i.e. Armed Forces; Prisons; Day-to-Day, In The Street, etc. The chaplain's role is to be able to read his audience. The difference between the chaplain and the pastor is when people call me pastor, everything that goes along with that title they are calling upon that ministry according to that role is how I have to speak to you. Pastor is personal; it's relationship, but as the chaplain I look over those things.

Question: What about the chaplains you have in your department?

Answer: When I reference the set NAVY instructions I am referencing the naval order that the chaplains, that govern the chaplains. In the set Navy instructions any religion that is recorded in the hall of congress I must recognize; that means across the board non-denominational, anything.

Question: When it comes to the tragic things of the community; how can we [community, clergy, etc.] be a help in that way?

Answer: Well, I understand through having trauma and tragedy in my life everything is working together for my good, their good. And even though it don't feel good, it don't smell good, it don't taste good, it's not appeasing to the flesh the bible is still true! Everything is working together for their good. It's my job to be a bridge to help them to the point that they can begin to see "it is for my good." So I don't look what helps me is because and one of my teachings I always say when you begin to wear the word of God as you wear your sunglasses. We're in southern California, sun is always shining in southern California; most of us have to get some sunglasses, because all day out in the sun our eyes get tired. And, so when you can put on the word of God and look through the word of God out into the world you begin to see the world as God sees it. So no matter what the traumatizing situation, tragic the situation is, in the family, outside the family, in the community I look at it through the eyes of God. I am compassionate, but I understand that there is a bigger purpose in what's going on. Everything is working together for the good of them who love God, and those who are called according to His purpose. I know there's a purpose for this. I know there's a purpose for that mother committing suicide. I know there's a purpose for this teenager running away from home. There is a purpose. And, know the bible says, "A hair doesn't fall from our head or a sparrow does not die without God knowing it" and there's a purpose for all things. And everything is as a professional counselor who deals in this area you don't allow anything to go inside of you that moves you from the position of the chaplain or a pastor because no matter what the issue, what the situation when I come in I represent the balancing grace of God. There's balance in the room. When I come into a room you can't speak from that corner [pointing to the corner of the room], and you can't speak from that corner [pointing to the opposite corner of the room] you must come to the center of the room. As you come to the center of the room there are some truths that you have to own up to [pointing to one corner], some truth that you have to own up to [pointing to the opposite corner] and we, not compromise our beliefs or who we are but we say the truth and the truth shall set you free ... that should bring us to the center of the room where we can begin to come to communicate. So whether I'm negotiating with a hostage, whether I am talking to a husband or a wife, or whether, no matter what I'm doing I'm coming into "where is the truth?" in this issue. I represent a balance. God gives us that authority to be His balancing grace.

Question: What life events led you to become a chaplain?

Answer: When you begin to cross the "T's" and dot the "I's" in the process of your life you begin to walk into your destiny. I had spent 22 years in the Marine Corps. I had been to Bible College; I started the City of Refuge in the City of Oceanside; I was actively involved in the marketplace meaning I am in the streets, in the marketplace. I had since spoke to a group of people in what we call Christ in City which there is a catholic church which is right across the street from City Hall. And what we started doing is every three months we had a service. The first service we acknowledged politicians, the second service we acknowledged law enforcement and we just acknowledge a certain group of people. The police chief at that time happened to attend one of our services. I was the keynote speaker; at the end he came and asked me for a card. Gave him a card just a run-of-the-mill, ordinary, old white man. A couple of days later I got a call and that caller asked me to come to the police department. Well, both my daughters had just got driver's licenses so I prayed; then I went to the police department. I got there and the sergeant at that time [can remember his name] sat me down and begin to explain the chaplaincy program and I let him finish and I told him I wanted no part of what he offered. And, he tried to convince me some more and I told him again I want no part of what you are offering; I am about to leave and he said, hold on you can't leave yet. So he went out the office came back and brought me and I walk into this big plush office and here is this, unassuming nerd of a white man who is actually the police chief. He says, I here you do not want my appointment as chaplain. Yes, sir you heard right. He says, why not? I spent 22 years in the Marine Corps, policy, procedures, protocol, I'm done! The only thing I am going to follow is my bible. I don't want the responsibility of being **under** any type of scrutiny. I'm going to say what I have to say; when I want to say it; how I want to say it and I don't want the hanging over my head, embarrassing the City or you or all of that stuff, I am done with all of that stuff! He said, will you try it for six months? I said, uh, you know what; let me think about that, and I will call you tomorrow or I will come back tomorrow and I will fill out your paperwork. What I did is I left and I called Bishop

Blake. I said, Bishop. I got this call and I just went on this little thing and I realize I am talking to a billionaire and tried to stop talking and he shared he reminded me of the story about Oral Roberts and being at the top section of the Crystal Cathedral … He reminded me of many of the classes we have taken and he says "opportunity does not knock; opportunity presents itself." He said after leaving Oral Roberts, I mean, after leaving the Crystal Cathedral. I came back and God opened up my eyes to opportunity. He says, so when you see an opportunity, you recognize an opportunity, have courage enough to go through the door. If you find out it is not your opportunity then walk back out the door. So I walked into the door and God began to move right-a-way. I went in did my life scan, my background check at 8:30 in the morning; at about 12:30 my stuff came back clear. It usually takes 7 days, 6 weeks. There was a gentleman who was an FBI chaplain who they did a background check on and his, it's been 10 days. His went in before mine; mine came back approved and they rushed me right through the system. Then, I was the first Black chaplain appointed to the City of Oceanside. That was in 2000. I am now the senior chaplain the Oceanside Police Department; chaplain of the District Attorneys Pastors Advisory Chaplain, the chair; I am chaplain at Camp Pendleton Base Brig; chaplain at Rainbow Conservation Camp. Camp Pendleton Brig at last Friday has 157 inmates. Rainbow Conservation Camp last Wednesday at 132 females. Donovan, Sunday, Donovan had 6583-5 inmates. [*sigh*] That's what I do as a chaplain.

Question: Did you attend a house of worship throughout your childhood?

Answer: I originally, my family is church family, ugh. I was drug to church; Church; church; church; church; church. I was cultivated in my social etiquette was taught in the church. And I got sick of church. I taught Sunday school at nine; preached my first message at twelve at the

A. M. E. church. At fifteen, I was running with the Black Unicorns, riding motorcycles and raising hell. Selling drugs etc. etc.

Question: What part of your job do you struggle with emotionally?

Answer: The part of my job I struggle with emotionally is the fact that when I know I am near the line that I can't cross over and that is when the pastor wants to come out and the chaplain actually is the working; the pastor wants to come out and the chaplain actually has the front door that's the struggling part. When I see a soul from the chaplain's perspective I am supposed to only do certain things, but there's some other practical things that a pastor would do that the chaplain can't do. So that is an emotional, a little emotion issue there.

Question: What part of your job brings you the most joy?

Answer: Everything about my job and then now this is where the chaplain and the pastor are cohabitating together. Because of what I do; who I am, the process of life and all the channels and everything that God has done; everything working together for our good making the scripture manifest and come completely important to me is the fact that life is an amusement park. My life is an amusement park. So you know how you feel; you know how you felt the first amusement park you went to. You know how you felt; feel when you are taking your children to an amusement park. You can't help from being a little excited yourself. So waking up with that type of amusement park excitement every day, meaning that that's what my life is. Now, the controlling portion or the part of government that God has established is that even thought my life is an amusement park, and I love the rollercoaster! And, I love the go-cart; and, I love the bumper cars; I don't like certain rides, but the authority of God in charge of our lives, my life even though it's an amusement park He tells me which ride that I need to get on. So the day when I would want to run to the rollercoaster, He says, get on the merry-go-round, and that's where the discipline comes in of yet having a life that's totally under the control of God, and totally exciting life where you can rest while you run.

Question: What makes you cry?

Answer: Well, what makes me cry is when I come into the chapel after driving 68 miles am I'm falling asleep behind the wheel because it's my third or fourth service for the evening and I drag into the chapel and I'm tired and I get into the office and I fall asleep and the guys come in and they look and they say chaplain, "you're tired" and I say, yeah and what makes me cry is when they take the service forward. They come they can do pray, they can do scripture, they do testimony and the very fact that they have been taught and have picked it up and they know how to do it. The tears of joy begin to stream down because they got it! And I know that I have put everything inside of them that I can and that they are prepared to go. When they get out they can go into a church and not feel estranged and know what's going on. Every basic, this is the basic structure of a church. We might do it as a black church more exuberantly and we are more charismatic about it but don't let my charisma and don't let my exuberance be the judge whether that's good church or not; because you might be the one that goes in and bring in and deliver what you do not see. So my greatest joy is to see that they got it!

Question: What frustrates and/or angers you?

Answer: What frustrates or angers me is just the opposite. When I have poured and poured and poured and poured and they come and ask me .... What frustrates me most is when I am in communication with someone, in a counseling session or actually seeing the work is done having to repeat myself. That is a challenge for me. Because, when I am trying to communicate, I am trying to articulate in a way that it's understood. I know when I get excited I must talk very slow; and I know that I must repeat it before it comes out. So when I have done that and especially when I've come to the point where I think that I need to reassure that this person understands I'll say, "Do you understand what I have said?"; "can you tell me what I have said?" In a counseling session when an individual has shared their side of what they are dealing with and sometimes I respond in a story that is scripture but sometimes I respond scripture then a story; nevertheless, when that person responds back and I can hear that he isn't/or she's not listening … it takes a whole lot of Jesus for me to.. That really frustrates me.

Question: What kind of education and training do you have that enables you to perform in this capacity?

Answer: I can say like this as men and women of God first there is a call. A Macedonia call; a clarion call; a clear call, that God has designed you for this work! And then, any person with any common sense would want to make full proof of his ministry. The doctor, who hears a call he goes to medical school. The lawyer goes to law school. Everybody in their profession needs some type of training. But I would, also, like to add there is the classroom, and there is just the basic life skills training that you get from the process of life. So, there is a meshing, a coming together of both of these areas all the time. Because if you have Harvard, Yale and Princeton and have no common sense, you are an educated fool! You got book knowledge, but that's all you have. You have to be able to be even-handed so that takes the process of life.

International Bible College, Practical Degree in Theology; an AA degree in Theology; Jubilee Bible College, I got moved up a little bit more; International Crisis Intervention, I am on National Board all; of your tragedy, trauma stuff; that deals with we have CPR in the United States Marine Corps that we use out in the field "Start the breathing, treat the shock; stop the bleeding." So the same thing works in the spirit when you're administering. So the process of life prepares you to take these things and mesh them together. I am chaplain and part of the International Conference of Police Chaplains; TQL Total Quality Leadership Training. I have been a leader of Marines for 22 years in some capacity. And, now I have collected all of my education of 22 years I did write some training for the USMC while in uniform, active duty. So at this point when I went back to New Dimension Bible College I already, when they did my assessment, I already had a Master's Degree in whatever direction I wanted to go. Instead of them giving me a Master's Degree they said, "You can buy, pay for your Masters and we'll get it to you. You don't have to step foot into the classroom, but because you have been on this continual process of self-education we would like for you to do a Master's continuation for your PhD." Which that is where I am going right now. But it's not the classroom, it's biblical, it's theology, its Christology, it's all of these things that God's. This is the ultimate book right here [pointing to the Holy Bible] because this is your science, your history, this is your poetry, your trigonometry, and this is your calculus. Everything is here but you must allow your life process and your secular education to bring you to the point that no matter what you talk about you are actually speaking from here [pointing to his heart] and you recognize your audience and you are able to captivate your audience because of your knowledge of biblical truths that you can apply in your life because this is logos, this is alive, this is God's word. And when you speak logos out of these lips of clay when it hits the ear it becomes Rhema. Rhema changes lives.

Question: What would you say to others considering Chaplaincy as a profession?

Answer: First of all the most important thing is you must be in sync with yourself. You must be one with God and have a real relationship with Him. Only then will you be able to minister as a chaplain. When at Donovan State

Prison I lead the Indian sweat circles. I am a spiritual advisor leading the Indian sweat circles. They call God "grandfather". They reverence grandfather and they believe that spirit grandfather is in the smoke. Whatever, no problem, that's why they smoke theses special tobaccos that represent "grandfather" well, whatever dude that's smoke, that's what floats your boat, let's do it, let's have a sweat circle. So you must be secure in who you are and secure in God's word so that you can communicate, and that you're not so thin-skinned your offended if someone does not believe the bible like you believe it. If you're thin-skinned and if you don't have it then you're going to get out there and you're going to be offended. If you are offended by it you could cause someone to stumble. And the bible says, "Do not be a stumbling block, or a rock of offense to anyone." So I would advise you to make sure that are comfortable in this word of God. And once you are comfortable in this word of God then I ask you to look out and you must find that if you are pursuing a career in the Navy you must find a denomination who is going to support you and who is going to endorse you to be a Naval chaplain. And if that is not the level that you want to be there are all types of law enforcement chaplaincies that's around; there is the Red Cross, a course that you can take, there are Sheriff's chaplains, Fire department, Medical, chaplains in businesses, that come and do once a week, spiritual advisory, but most of all you must be centered in who you are.

Question: What is the role of a chaplain apart from the armed forces or institution and what is that chaplain's role between communities and police department?

Answer: Basically the law enforcement chaplain or the chaplain of the community has to have a relationship with his police chief and the community and that would establish a relationship so that when something happens there is a proactive connection with the police chief or law enforcement versus a reactive connection. Because if it is totally a reactive connection that means the only time that you as a man of God, as a chaplain would see or communicate with your police chief would be during a crisis. But when you have a proactive relationship with your police chief or law enforcement that means that you are communicating with him; he knows you; you know him so anytime that he feels that he is at a deficit, feeling a weak point in his relationships with the community he will call on that chaplain or that person to be the bridge between him and the community and vice-versa. If Mother Jones' grandson got picked up and Mother Jones was bringing that young man to church but now he's just a little bit misguided, and a little bit of influence to the wrong way. So from the community side of the house me as the chaplain goes in and says 'hey' chief this is Mother Jones' boy; District Attorney this is Mother Jones' boy so why don't you order him to come back to the church and put him under the charge of the church by your order and then that would give us some control over him because he's been court ordered or advised, because the court cannot order him to go to a specific institution, but the court can advise him to seek religious, spiritual counseling and guidance. So the relationship between chaplain and community and police department is very and in that aspect every clergy, every pastor, and I'm talking senior pastor must have that slight bit of chaplaincy within him that he would leave out of his four walls, church, and establish a relationship with law enforcement in his city.

Summation

Real People Called to an Extraordinary Ministry of Presence

Ecclesiastical endorsement legal ministry license ordination Chaplaincy and Ministry Training

Romans 12:4-8 (NIV) "Just as each of us has one body with many members, and these members do not all have the same function, so in Christ we who are many form one body, and each member belongs to all the others. We have different gifts, according to the grace given us. If a man's gift is prophesying, let him use it in proportion to his faith. If it is serving, let him serve; if it is teaching, let him teach; if it is encouraging, let him encourage; if it is contributing to the needs of others, let him give generously; if it is leadership, let him govern diligently; if it is showing mercy, let him do it cheerfully."

The members of Chaplain Fellowship Ministries are ordained as nondenominational ministers and chaplains by our ordaining body of senior chaplains. We are a one of a kind ministry of presence with members and affiliate ministries worldwide. We come from all faith groups, ethnic, gender and educational backgrounds, Chaplain Fellowship with the Lords' guidance has been molded and shaped after the Ministry of Jesus and we are growing by leaps and bounds everyday folks. We are looking for real people who are serious about their calling. The members of Chaplain Fellowship Ministries are very real hard working people with the heart and compassion to reach out to the needy and lost all over the United States and around the world. (Gibson, 2010)

James 1:12 "Happy are those who remain faithful under trials, because when they succeed in passing such a test, they will receive as their reward the life which God has promised to those who love him." (GNT)

Chaplain Fellowship is about the Great Commission. Do you feel like you are being called to do something that will make a difference in life, but you don't know where to start? I think that maybe we have all felt that call at some point in our lives. Becoming ordained as a Chaplain and Minister will take you far beyond your wildest imagination and it will make you a much larger person in the spirit of the Lord, than you ever dreamed you could be. As Chaplains and Ministers if we see someone in need and have the ability to help them and don't, how can we say that the love of Jesus abides in us? Never forget that what we go after here on earth, determines where we go in the hereafter. We make a living from what we get, but we make a life from what we give. Anyone can give without loving, but no one can love without giving. (Gibson, 2010) **Proverbs 11:25** "Be generous, and you will be prosperous. Help others, and you will be helped." (GNT) Those who are good are rewarded here on earth, so you can be sure that wicked and sinful people will be punished.

Chaplain Donald Gibson shares that Chaplain Fellowship Ministries is internationally recognized as a faith based nondenominational ministry of presence that offers everyone including the everyday hard working man or woman an opportunity to serve in the position of an ordained Chaplain and Minister through specific ministry programs. Chaplain Fellowship offers ordination, ecclesiastical endorsements and certifications in your chosen field of ministry, thereby, allowing anyone who feels God has called them to be able to minister at some level as an ordained Chaplain and Minister. Our Mission is to ordain, qualify, equip, and offer training and to officially recognize those seeking legal ministry license, ordination, endorsement and certification documentation as ministers, pastors, priests and chaplains. (Gibson, 2010)

We know by building and strengthening our communities and proclaiming the Gospel of Jesus to the world at large we are doing what He has called us to do. Jesus has poured out His Spirit upon us, we are to help the lost who are seeking salvation, we are to help those seeking healing for the spirit soul and body with the anointing that rests upon each of us in the name of Jesus. (Gibson, 2010)

James 1:27 "What God the Father considers to be pure and genuine religion is this: to take care of orphans and widows in their suffering and to keep oneself from being corrupted by the world." (GNT)

Chaplain Fellowship Ministries is an outreach ministry of presence dedicated to recruiting those who have been called into the Lord's ministry. Chaplain Fellowship Ministries will not judge you, belittle you or criticize you for your past. Please understand it takes all of us to get the job done, just as Jesus recruited many from different backgrounds including educational. It does not take a college graduate to walk into a biker bar full of 1%ers, it takes a biker who has been there, it takes a hard-core ordained biker Chaplain. Nursing home chaplaincy or ministry takes a chaplain who is ordained and has compassion, love and understanding, it takes those who have the love of Jesus in their hearts. It requires someone who knows how to listen, and many times someone to just be there with them when they are dying, the thought of dying alone is very scary for senior citizens. Who better to work with our returning troops or veterans of other wars than veteran who are chaplains themselves that have been there and understand their pain, suffering, fears and disappointments? (Gibson, 2010)

Psalm 41:1-3 "Blessed is he who considers the poor; the Lord will deliver him in time of trouble. The Lord will preserve him and keep him alive, and he will be blessed on the earth; He will not deliver him to the will of his enemies. The Lord will strengthen him on his bed of illness; He will sustain him on his sickbed." (ESV)

Our Lord wants to transform our corrupted nature into divine nature. When we repent and sincerely want to change, He takes a "piece" of Himself, His Spirit, His unselfish nature, His mind, and His pure love and places that inside our minds to change how we think and feel. (Gibson, 2010)

The picture featured in this article cited is of a very real person and the best example we have to prove the need for nursing home Chaplains; no one should ever be treated the way depicted in the photo. When Chaplains make regular visits to nursing homes, it cuts down on this type of mistreatment. Not all nursing homes have this type of abuse, but there are many that do. This little lady is a child of God, and there is no doubt that there is a special place in Heaven for her. This type of abuse is a disgrace and we should all be ashamed to allow such treatment of our senior citizen. As legally ordained Chaplains we CAN make a difference in this world, we just need to get out there and do it. All it takes is good hearted people who have compassion, mercy, kindness, love and understanding. If you don't want to be a legally ordained chaplain or minister, please just do something in your life to make a difference in the lives of those who are hurting, suffering, lost everything or have nothing and nowhere to turn. Folks it is up to us! (Gibson, 2010)

James 2:13 "For judgment is without mercy to the one who has shown no mercy. Mercy triumphs over judgment." (ESV) Does anyone not want a merciful judgment from God, before whom all must stand?

When you begin your work as an ordained chaplain and minister you can be confident that the Lord, who has already started a good work in you, will complete it. Please never let anyone tell you that you are not good enough for the Lord's ministry, or that the Lord has not called you into ministry. There is no human being on this earth who has the right to judge who has or have not been called. We all need Jesus as our Lord and Savior in our everyday lives. He is the one who can lift us above the degrading forces of evil in the world that tries to tell us we are not good enough. It is Jesus who holds all things together, including our lives. Become a member and receive your God given right to ordination and license as a legal member of the clergy. Take a leap of faith, and watch your whole world, and the way you see thing, literally transform before your very eyes. (Gibson, 2010)

Galatians 1:6-9; 3:1 "Spiritual enemies also include false teachers. We must be extremely cautious about whom we listen to. Never let anyone tell you that you are not good enough, or smart enough, to follow the Lords' calling in your lives."

Those Who Share In His Suffering Shall Also Share In His Glory! We believe all Christians have been given spiritual gifts to fulfill their callings. Ministry ordination is a spiritual gift and calling directly from God and is not to be taken lightly. He chooses to call who he will, or to use any instrument, to accomplish His will. Jesus said, I will build My church and the gates of hell will not prevail against it. Never let any man or woman stop you from doing what you have been called to do. When you act upon your calling, you then become a member of HIS Ministry. (Gibson, 2010)

As Chaplains the compassion, mercy, understanding and love we show for those in need will be the only bible many will ever get a chance to see. A wise man once said that our decisions determine our direction, and our direction determines our destiny. Let your direction be true, and let your destiny be one of greatness for the glory of God's kingdom. No one knows when Jesus will return; maybe it will be today or maybe in a 1000 years. His return is something we have no control over. The only control we have in this life is this moment in time, so let us live every moment as if it is our last, for the glory of His kingdom. (Gibson, 2010)

Matthew 25:21 "His lord said unto him, Well done, thou good and faithful servant: thou hast been faithful over a few things, I will make thee ruler over many things: enter thou into the joy of thy lord." (KJV)

Chaplains are ministers called to serve God's people as commissioned by the sacred Word of God. In Christian grace and duty Chaplains respond with love and compassion to people's needs in their whole existence.

Chaplains embrace the understanding that human beings are created in the image of God with uniqueness and freedom to think, act and feel. When we do our best, the word of God is true, He will do the rest. (Gibson, 2010)

2 Corinthians 4:1 "God in his mercy has given us this work to do, and so we do not become discouraged." (GNT) With our Lord and Savior beside us we go into each day as we are, just as our Lord went into each day ready to serve, to seek and to save those who are lost; to look for opportunity to love and to heal. With our Lord and Savior beside us we can love just as we are, unconditionally, without regard for ourselves sacrificially and without hesitation. By seeking our Lord and Savior fully, honestly and humbly, we can go through each day, just as we are. (Gibson, 2010)

Galatians 6:9-10 "And let us not grow weary while doing good, for in due season we shall reap if we do not lose heart. Therefore, as we have opportunity, let us do good to all, especially to those who are of the household of faith [fellow believers]." (NKJV) Chaplain Fellowship offers training to anyone who feels they need it. For all those who want to seek training on their own they might find the following training materials to be helpful: Chaplain Books and Training Materials, Wedding Manuals, Funeral Manuals, Hospital Visitation Manuals, How - To Manuals, Minister's Manuals, Minister's Service Manual, Premarital Guidance, Ordination, Crisis Chaplaincy, Anger Management, On Death and Dying, Endorsing Agency, Emotional Freedom Techniques, Grief Recovery Workbook, Impact Ministries, Crisis Intervention, Faith Based Training, Start a Church, Counseling, Military Chaplaincy, Helping People Through Grief, Pastoral Care, Women in Ministry, Aging, Spirituality and Religion, Becoming Ordained, Restorative Therapy, Anger Management, The Principles of Prison Ministry, Ordaining, Ecclesiastical Endorsement, Ministry to the Incarcerated, Prison Ministry, Understanding Prison Culture Inside and Out, and a lot more. (Gibson, 2010)

CFMI Anger Management is a department of Chaplain Fellowship Ministries an official continuing education provider for the following. The Texas State Board of Social Work Examiners, The Texas State Board of Examiners of Professional Counselors and the Texas State Board of Examiners of Marriage and Family Therapists. CFMI Anger Management has been approved by the Bell and Lampasas county departments of probation to provide court ordered anger management. (Gibson, 2010)

Matthew 7:15 "Many have come preaching Christ for personal gain. Some have come to devour the very people they are trying to reach, all in the name of Christ. *Jesus warned us; Don't let anyone stop you from following your calling.*"

Someone once told said that if we give a man a fish, we feed him for one day, but if we teach him to fish, we feed him for a lifetime. God carries out His plan through those obedient to Him in spite of their human frailties. (Gibson, 2010)

Irrational ideas foster irrational behavior. How we think controls the way we live and how we relate to other people. Our thoughts will influence our decisions and our actions. Ultimately, we are what we think. (Gibson, 2010)

The Zondervan Corporation gives us Scriptural references that support the work of the chaplain in offering strength, hope, assurance, courage and promises.

PAUL » Escapes to Derbe, where he preaches the gospel, and returns to Lystra, and to Iconium, and to Antioch, strengthens the souls of the disciples, exhorts them to continue in the faith, and helps to appoint elders (Acts 14:19-23 KJV)

Acts 14:19-23 And there came thither certain Jews from Antioch and Iconium, who persuaded the people, and having stoned Paul, drew him out of the city, supposing he had been dead. [20]Howbeit, as the disciples stood round about him, he rose up, and came into the city: and the next day he departed with Barnabas to Derbe. [21]And when they had preached the gospel to that city, and had taught many, they returned again to Lystra, and to Iconium, and Antioch, [22]Confirming the souls of the disciples, and exhorting them to continue in the faith, and that we must through much tribulation enter into the kingdom of God. [23]And when they had ordained them elders in every church, and had prayed with fasting, they commended them to the Lord, on whom they believed.

PAUL » Chooses Silas as his companion, and passes through Syria and Cilicia, strengthening the congregations (Acts 15:36-41 KJV)

Acts 15:36-41 And some days after Paul said unto Barnabas, Let us go again and visit our brethren in every city where we have preached the word of the LORD, and see how they do. [37]And Barnabas determined to take with them John, whose surname was Mark. [38]But Paul thought not good to take him with them, who departed from them from Pamphylia, and went not with them to the work.

And the contention was so sharp between them, that they departed asunder one from the other: and so Barnabas took Mark, and sailed unto Cyprus; [40]And Paul chose Silas, and departed, being recommended by the brethren unto the grace of God. [41]And he went through Syria and Cilicia, confirming the churches.

PAUL » Visits Ephesus, where he leaves Aquila and Priscilla; enters into a synagogue, where he reasons with the Jews; starts on his return trip to Jerusalem; visits Caesarea; crosses over the country of Galatia and Phrygia, strengthening the disciples (Acts 18:18-23 KJV)

Acts 18:18-23 And Paul after this tarried there yet a good while, and then took his leave of the brethren, and sailed thence into Syria, and with him Priscilla and Aquila; having shorn his head in Cenchrea: for he had a vow. [19]And he came to Ephesus, and left them there: but he himself entered into the synagogue, and reasoned with the Jews. [20]When they desired him to tarry longer time with them, he consented not; [21]But bade them farewell, saying, I must by all means keep this feast that cometh in Jerusalem: but I will return again unto you, if God will. And he sailed from Ephesus. [22]And when he had landed at Caesarea, and gone up, and saluted the church, he went down to Antioch. [23]And after he had spent some time there, he departed, and went over all the country of Galatia and Phrygia in order, strengthening all the disciples.

PAUL » Proceeds to Macedonia after strengthening the congregations in that region; comes into Greece and lives for three months; returns through Macedonia, accompanied by Sopater, Aristarchus, Secundus, Gaius, Timothy, Tychicus, and Trophimus (Acts 20:1-6 KJV)

Acts 20:1 And after the uproar was ceased, Paul called unto him the disciples, and embraced them, and departed for to go into Macedonia. [2]And when he had gone over those parts, and had given them much exhortation, he came into Greece, [3]And there abode three months. And when the Jews laid wait for him, as he was about to sail into Syria, he purposed to return through Macedonia. [4]And there accompanied him into Asia Sopater of Berea; and of the Thessalonians, Aristarchus and Secundus; and Gaius of Derbe, and Timotheus; and of Asia, Tychicus and Trophimus. [5]These going before tarried for us at Troas. [6]And we sailed away from Philippi after the days of unleavened bread, and came unto them to Troas in five days; where we abode seven days.

POWER » OF CHRIST » Strengthened by (Philippians 4:13; 2 Timothy 4:17 KJV)

Philippians 4:13 I can do all things through Christ which strengtheneth me.

Expresses contentment in every condition of life. It is a good work to succour and help a good minister in trouble. The nature of true Christian sympathy is not only to feel concern for our friends in their troubles, but to do what we can to help them. The apostle was often in bonds, imprisonments, and necessities; but in all, he learned to be content, to bring his mind to his condition, and make the best of it. Pride, unbelief, vain hankering after something we have not got, and fickle disrelish of present things, make men discontented even under favorable circumstances. Let us pray for patient submission and hope when we are abased; for humility and a heavenly mind when exalted. It is a special grace to have an equal temper of mind always. And in a low state not to lose our comfort in God, nor distrust his providence, nor take any wrong course for our own supply. In a prosperous condition not to be proud, or secure, or worldly. This is a harder lesson than the other; for the temptations of fullness and prosperity are more than those of affliction and want. The apostle had no design to urge them to give more, but to encourage such kindness as will meet a glorious reward hereafter. Through Christ we have grace to do what is good, and through him we must expect the reward; and as we have all things by him, let us do all things for him, and to his glory. (Henry, 1706)

2 Timothy 4:17 Notwithstanding the Lord stood with me, and strengthened me; that by me the preaching might be fully known, and that all the Gentiles might hear: and I was delivered out of the mouth of the lion.

The duties which become sound doctrine. There is as much danger from false brethren, as from open enemies. It is dangerous having to do with those who would be enemies to such a man as Paul. The Christians at Rome were forward to meet him, Acts 28, but when there seemed to be a danger of suffering with him, then all forsook him. God might justly be angry with them, but he prays God to forgive them. The apostle was delivered out of the mouth of the lion, that is, of Nero, or some of his judges. If the Lord stands by us, he will strengthen us in difficulties and dangers, and his presence will more than supply every one's absence. (Henry, 1706)

POWER » OF GOD » Is the source of all strength (1 Chronicles 29:12; Psalms 68:35 KJV)

1 Chronicles 29:12 Both riches and honour come of thee, and thou reignest over all; and in thine hand is power and might; and in thine hand it is to make great, and to give strength unto all.

Hezekiah's good reign in Judah. When Hezekiah came to the crown, he applied at once to work reform. Those who begin with God begin at the right end of their work, and it will prosper accordingly. Those that turn their backs upon God's ordinances may truly be said to forsake God himself. There are still such neglects, if the word be not duly read and opened, for that was signified by the lighting the lamps, and also if prayers and praise be not offered up, for that was signified by the burning incense. Neglect of God's worship was the cause of the calamities they had lain under. The Lord alone can prepare the heart of man for vital godliness: when much good is done in a little time, the glory must be ascribed to him; and all who love him or the souls of men, will rejoice therein. Let those that do good work, learn to do it well. (Henry, 1706)

Psalm 68:35 O God, thou art terrible out of thy holy places: the God of Israel is he that giveth strength and power unto his people. Blessed be God.

The glory and grace of God. God is to be admired and adored with reverence and godly fear, by all that attend in his holy places. The God of Israel gives strength and power unto his people. Through Christ strengthening us we can do all things, not otherwise; therefore he must have the glory of all we do, with our humble thanks for enabling us to do it, and for accepting the work of his hands in us. (Henry, 1706)

POWER » OF GOD » Strengthened by (Ephesians 6:10; Colossians 1:11 KJV)

Ephesians 6:10 Finally, my brethren, be strong in the Lord, and in the power of his might.

All Christians are to put on spiritual armor against the enemies of their souls. Spiritual strength and courage are needed for our spiritual warfare and suffering. Those who would prove themselves to have true grace must aim at all grace; and put on the whole armor of God, which he prepares and bestows. The Christian armor is made to be worn; and there is no putting off our armor till we have done our warfare, and finished our course. The combat is not against human enemies, nor against our own corrupt nature only; we have to do with an enemy who has a thousand ways of beguiling unstable souls. The devils assault us in the things that belong to our souls, and labor to deface the heavenly image in our hearts. We must resolve by God's grace, not to yield to Satan. Resist him, and he will flee. If we give way, he will get ground. If we distrust either our cause, or our Leader, or our armor, we give him advantage. The different parts of the armor of heavy-armed soldiers, who had to sustain the fiercest assaults of the enemy, are here described. There is none for the back; nothing to defend those who turn back in the Christian warfare. Truth, or sincerity, is the girdle. This girds on all the other pieces of our armor, and is first mentioned. There can be no religion without sincerity. The righteousness of Christ, imputed to us, is a breastplate against the arrows of Divine wrath. The righteousness of Christ implanted in us, fortifies the heart against the attacks of Satan. Resolution must be as greaves, or armor to our legs; and to stand their ground or to march forward in rugged paths, the feet must be shod with the preparation of the gospel of peace.

Motives to obedience, amidst trials, must be drawn from a clear knowledge of the gospel. Faith is all in all in an hour of temptation. Faith, as relying on unseen objects, receiving Christ and the benefits of redemption, and so deriving grace from him, is like a shield, a defense every way. The devil is the wicked one. Violent temptations, by which the soul is set on fire of hell, are darts Satan shoots at us. Also, hard thoughts of God, and as to ourselves. Faith applying the word of God and the grace of Christ quenches the darts of temptation. Salvation must be our helmet. A good hope of salvation, a Scriptural expectation of victory, will purify the soul, and keep it from being defiled by Satan. To the Christian armed for defense in battle, the apostle recommends only one weapon of attack; but it is enough, the sword of the Spirit, which is the word of God. It subdues and mortifies evil desires and blasphemous thoughts as they rise within; and answers unbelief and error as they assault from without. A single text, well understood, and rightly applied, at once destroys a temptation or an objection, and subdues the most formidable adversary. Prayer must fasten all the other parts of our Christian armor. There are other duties of religion, and of our stations in the world, but we must keep up times of prayer. Though set and solemn prayer may not be seasonable when other duties are to be done, yet short pious prayers darted out, always are so. We must use holy thoughts in our ordinary course. A vain heart will be vain in prayer. We must pray with all kinds of prayer, public, private, and secret; social and solitary; solemn and sudden: with all the parts of prayer; confession of sin, petition for mercy, and thanksgiving for favors received. And we must do it by the grace of God the Holy Spirit, in dependence on, and according to, his teaching. We must preserve in particular requests, notwithstanding discouragements. We must pray, not for ourselves only, but for all saints. Our enemies are mighty, and we are without strength, but our

Redeemer is almighty, and in the power of his mighty we may overcome. Wherefore we must stir up ourselves. Have not we, when God has called, often neglected to answer? Let us think upon these things, and continue our prayers with patience. (Henry, 1706)

Colossians 1:11 Strengthened with all might, according to his glorious power, unto all patience and longsuffering with joyfulness;

Prays for their fruitfulness in spiritual knowledge. The apostle was constant in prayer, that the believers might be filled with the knowledge of God's will, in all wisdom. Good words will not do without good works. He, who undertakes to give strength to his people, is a God of power, and of glorious power. The blessed Spirit is the author of this. In praying for spiritual strength, we are not straitened, or confined in the promises, and should not be so in our hopes and desires. The grace of God in the hearts of believers is the power of God; and there is glory in this power. The special use of this strength was for sufferings. There is work to be done, even when we are suffering. Amidst all their trials they gave thanks to the Father of our Lord Jesus, whose special grace fitted them to partake of the inheritance provided for the saints. To bring about this change, those were made willing subjects of Christ, who were slaves of Satan. All who are designed for heaven hereafter are prepared for heaven now. Those who have the inheritance of sons, have the education of sons, and the disposition of sons. By faith in Christ they enjoyed this redemption, as the purchase of his atoning blood, whereby forgiveness of sins and all other spiritual blessings were bestowed. Surely then we shall deem it a favor to be delivered from Satan's kingdom and brought into that of Christ, knowing that all trials will soon end, and that every believer will be found among those who come out of great tribulation. (Henry, 1706)

POWER » OF THE HOLY SPIRIT » Strengthened by (Ephesians 3:16 KJV)

Ephesians 3:16 That he would grant you, according to the riches of his glory, to be strengthened with might by his Spirit in the inner man;

He prays for the Ephesians. The apostle seems to be more anxious lest the believers should be discouraged and faint upon his tribulations, than for what he himself had to bear. He asks for spiritual blessings, which are the best blessings. Strength from the Spirit of God in the inner man; strength in the soul; the strength of faith, to serve God, and to do our duty. If the law of Christ is written in our hearts, and the love of Christ is shed abroad there, then Christ dwells there. Where his Spirit dwells, there he dwells. We should desire that good affections may be fixed in us. And how desirable to have a fixed sense of the love of God in Christ to our souls! How powerfully the apostle speaks of the love of Christ! The breadth shows its extent to all nations and ranks; the length that it continues from everlasting to everlasting; the depth, its saving those who are sunk into the depths of sin and misery; the height, its raising them up to heavenly happiness and glory. Those who receive grace for grace from Christ's fullness may be said to be filled with the fullness of God. Should not this satisfy man? Must he needs fill himself with a thousand trifles, fancying thereby completing his happiness? (Henry, 1706)

PRAYER » ANSWERED » Samson, asking for strength (Judges 16:28-30 KJV)

Judges 16:28-30 And Samson called unto the LORD, and said, O Lord God, remember me, I pray thee, and strengthen me, I pray thee, only this once, O God, that I may be at once avenged of the Philistines for my two eyes. [29]And Samson took hold of the two middle pillars upon which the house stood, and on which it was borne up, of the one with his right hand, and of the other with his left. [30]And

Samson said, Let me die with the Philistines. And he bowed himself with all his might; and the house fell upon the lords, and upon all the people that were therein. So the dead which he slew at his death were more than they which he slew in his life.

WAR » FIGURATIVE » Strengthened by God in (Psalms 20:2;27:14; Isaiah 41:10 KJV) Psalm 20:2 Send thee help from the sanctuary, and strengthen thee out of Zion;

Psalm 27:14 Wait on the LORD: be of good courage, and he shall strengthen thine heart: wait, I say, on the LORD.

His desire toward God, and expectation from him. Wherever the believer is, he can find a way to the throne of grace by prayer. God calls us by his Spirit, by his word, by his worship, and by special providences, merciful and afflicting. When we are foolishly making court to lying vanities, God is, in love to us, calling us to seek our own mercies in him. The call is general, to Seek ye my face; but we must apply it to ourselves, I will seek it. The word does us no good, when we do not ourselves accept the exhortation: a gracious heart readily answers to the call of a gracious God, being made willing in the day of his power. The psalmist requests the favor of the Lord; the continuance of his presence with him; the benefit of Divine guidance, and the benefit of Divine protection. God's time to help those that trust in him is, when all other helpers fail. He is a surer and better Friend than earthly parents are, or can be. What was the belief which supported the psalmist? That he should see the goodness of the Lord. There is nothing like the believing hope of eternal life, the foresights of that glory, and foretastes of those pleasures, to keep us from fainting under all calamities. In the mean time he should be strengthened to bear up under his burdens. Let us look unto the suffering Savior, and pray in faith, not to be delivered into the hands of our enemies. Let us encourage each other to wait on the Lord, with patient expectation, and fervent prayer. (Henry, 1706)

Isaiah 41:10 Fear thou not; for I am with thee: be not dismayed; for I am thy God: I will strengthen thee; yea, I will help thee; yea, I will uphold thee with the right hand of my righteousness.

WAR » FIGURATIVE » Strengthened by Christ in (2 Corinthians 12:9; 2 Timothy 4:17 KJV)

2 Corinthians 12:9 And he said unto me, My grace is sufficient for thee: for my strength is made perfect in weakness. Most gladly therefore will I rather glory in my infirmities, that the power of Christ may rest upon me.

Which were improved to his spiritual advantage? The apostle gives an account of the method God took to keep him humble, and to prevent his being lifted up above measure, on account of the visions and revelations he had. We are not told what this thorn in the flesh was, whether some great trouble, or some great temptation. But God often brings this good out of evil that the reproaches of our enemies help to hide pride from us. If God loves us, he will keep us from being exalted above measure; and spiritual burdens are ordered to cure spiritual pride. This thorn in the flesh is said to be a messenger of Satan which he sent for evil; but God designed it, and overruled it for good. Prayer is a salve for every sore, a remedy for every malady; and when we are afflicted with thorns in the flesh, we should give ourselves to prayer. If an answer be not given to the first prayer, nor to the second, we are to continue praying. Troubles are sent to teach us to pray; and are continued, to teach us to continue instant in prayer. (Henry, 1706)

Though God accepts the prayer of faith, yet he does not always give what is asked for: as he sometimes grants in wrath, so he sometimes denies in love. When God does not take away our troubles and temptations, yet, if he gives grace enough for us, we have no reason to complain. Grace signifies the good-will of God towards us, and that is enough to enlighten and enliven us, sufficient to strengthen and comfort in all afflictions and distresses. His strength is made perfect in our weakness. Thus his grace is manifested and magnified. When we are weak in ourselves, then we are strong in the grace of our Lord Jesus Christ; when we feel that we are weak in ourselves, and then we go to Christ, receive strength from him, and enjoy most the supplies of Divine strength and grace. (Henry, 1706)

2 Timothy 4:17 Notwithstanding the Lord stood with me, and strengthened me; that by me the preaching might be fully known, and that all the Gentiles might hear: and I was delivered out of the mouth of the lion.

The duties which become sound doctrine. There is as much danger from false brethren, as from open enemies. It is dangerous having to do with those who would be enemies to such a man as Paul. The Christians at Rome were forward to meet him, Acts 28, but when there seemed to be a danger of suffering with him, then all forsook him. God might justly be angry with them, but he prays God to forgive them. The apostle was delivered out of the mouth of the lion, that is, of Nero, or some of his judges. If the Lord stands by us, he will strengthen us in difficulties and dangers, and his presence will more than supply every one's absence.

(Henry, 1706)Called » AMBASSADORS FOR CHRIST (2 Corinthians 5:20 KJV) 2 Corinthians 5:20 Now then we are ambassadors for Christ, as though God did beseech you by us: we pray you in Christ's stead, be ye reconciled to God.

The necessity of regeneration, and of reconciliation with God through Christ. The renewed man acts upon new principles, by new rules, with new ends, and in new company. The believer is created anew; his heart is not merely set right, but a new heart is given him. He is the workmanship of God, created in Christ Jesus unto good works. Though the same as a man, he is changed in his character and conduct. These words must and do mean more than an outward reformation. The man who formerly saw no beauty in the Savior that he should desire him; now loves him above all things. The heart of the unregenerate is filled with enmity against God, and God is justly offended with him. Yet there may be reconciliation. Our offended God has reconciled us to himself by Jesus Christ. By the inspiration of God, the Scriptures were written, which are the word of reconciliation; showing that peace has been made by the cross, and how we may be interested therein. Though God cannot lose by the quarrel, nor gain by the peace, yet he beseeches sinners to lay aside their enmity, and accept the salvation he offers. Christ knew no sin. He was made Sin; not a sinner, but Sin, a Sin-offering, a Sacrifice for sin. The end and design of all this was, that we might be made the righteousness of God in him, might be justified freely by the grace of God through the redemption which is in Christ Jesus. Can any lose, labor, or suffer too much for Him, who gave his beloved Son to be the Sacrifice for their sins, that they might be made the righteousness of God in him? (Henry, 1706)

Called » ANGELS OF THE CHURCH (Revelation 1:20; 2:1 KJV)

Revelation 1:20 The mystery of the seven stars which thou sawest in my right hand, and the seven golden candlesticks. The seven stars are the angels of the seven churches: and the seven candlesticks which thou sawest are the seven churches.

Revelation 2:1 Unto the angel of the church of Ephesus write; These things saith he that holdeth the seven stars in his right hand, who walketh in the midst of the seven golden candlesticks;

Upon which all honor is ascribed to him, as worthy to open it. These churches were in such different states as to purity of doctrine and the power of godliness, that the words of Christ to them will always suit the cases of other churches, and professors. Christ knows and observes their state; though in heaven, yet he walks in the midst of his churches on earth, observing what is wrong in them, and what they want. The church of Ephesus is commended for diligence in duty. Christ keeps an account of every hour's work his servants do for him, and their labor shall not be in vain in the Lord. But it is not enough that we are diligent; there must be bearing patience, and there must be waiting patience. And though we must show all meekness to all men, yet we must show just zeal against their sins. The sin Christ charged this church with, is, not the having left and forsaken the object of love, but having lost the fervent degree of it that at first appeared. Christ is displeased with his people, when he sees them grow remiss and cold toward him. Surely this mention in Scripture, of Christians forsaking their first love, reproves those who speak of it with carelessness, and thus try to excuse indifference and sloth in themselves and others; our Savior considers this indifference as sinful. They must repent: they must be grieved and ashamed for their sinful declining, and humbly confess it in the sight of God. They must endeavor to recover their first zeal, tenderness, and seriousness, and must pray as earnestly, and watch as diligently, as when they first set out in the ways of God. If the presence of Christ's grace and Spirit is slighted, we may expect the presence of his displeasure. Encouraging mention is made of what was good among them. Indifference as to truth and error, good and evil, may be called charity and meekness, but it is not so; and it is displeasing to Christ. The Christian life is warfare against sin, Satan, the world, and the flesh. We must never yield to our spiritual enemies, and then we shall have a glorious triumph and reward. All who persevere shall derive from Christ, as the Tree of life, perfection and confirmation in holiness and happiness, not in the earthly paradise, but in the heavenly. This is a figurative expression, taken from the account of the Garden of Eden, denoting the pure, satisfactory, and eternal joys of heaven; and the looking forward to them in this world, by faith, communion with Christ, and the consolations of the Holy Spirit. Believers, take your wrestling life here, and expect and look for a quiet life hereafter; but not till then: the word of God never promises quietness and complete freedom from conflict here. (Henry, 1706)

Called » APOSTLES (Luke 6:13; Revelation 18:20 KJV)

Luke 6:13 And when it was day, he called unto him his disciples: and of them he chose twelve, whom also he named apostles;

The apostles chosen. We often think one half hour a great deal to spend in meditation and secret prayer, but Christ was whole nights engaged in these duties. In serving God, our great care should be not to lose time, but to make the end of one good duty the beginning of another. The twelve apostles are here named; never were men so privileged, yet one of them had a devil, and proved a traitor. Those who have not faithful preaching near them had better travel far than be without it. It is indeed worthwhile to go a great way to hear the word of Christ, and to go out of the way of other business for it. They came to be cured by him, and he healed them. There is a fullness of grace in Christ, and healing virtue in him, ready to go out from him that is enough for all, enough for each. Men regard the diseases of the body as greater evils than those of their souls; but the Scripture teaches us differently. (Henry, 1706)

Revelation 18:20 Rejoice over her, thou heaven, and ye holy apostles and prophets; for God hath avenged you on her.

The church called upon to rejoice in her utter ruin.
That, which is matter of rejoicing to the servants of God on
earth, is matter of rejoicing to the angels in heaven. The
apostles, who are honored and daily worshipped at Rome in
an idolatrous manner, will rejoice in her fall. The fall of
Babylon was an act of God's justice. And because it was a
final ruin, this enemy should never molest them anymore;
of this they were assured by a sign. Let us take warning
from the things which brought others to destruction, and let
us set our affections on things above, when we consider the
changeable nature of earthly things. (Henry, 1706)

Called » APOSTLES OF JESUS CHRIST (Titus 1:1
KJV)
Titus 1:1 Paul, a servant of God, and an apostle of Jesus
Christ, according to the faith of God's elect, and the
acknowledging of the truth which is after godliness;

Greeting How many of us really know who we are and
why we are here? Of course, we all have names and our
own personal histories. We have goals, dreams and
characteristics which we feel give us a special identity, and
these things are certainly to be valued. But when we think
about reason for being, personal identity and meaning in
life, do we do so with God and his will in mind? (Henry,
1706)

The letter to Titus lays that challenge, among others, before
us today. Much of the letter encourages rather ordinary
believers, who occupy all walks of life, to consider their
lives in every facet as an expression of the will of God. In
fact, once life is considered in this way, the thought of
"ordinariness" departs from Christian thinking about life.
No matter what path God has given us to walk, we are
intended to be a vital piece in God's missionary plan to
reach the rest of the world. Each "piece" has meaning, each
human life has inestimable value and usefulness to God,

and this realization is a tremendous source of joy, satisfaction and peace. But to comprehend this, we may need to make some adjustments in the way we view life. Let's begin, then, with a look at how Paul defined his own life. Although he was an apostle, the pattern of his thinking ought also to be ours. (Henry, 1706)

As he does in the opening greeting of 1Timothy, Paul again identifies formally his status and his office and then identifies and blesses the intended recipient. In comparison with 1 Timothy, however, the apostle, using very compact language, describes in more detail his Christian *raison d'être*. This sets the tone and introduces the main theme of the letter. The Sender (Henry, 1706)

Called » DEFENDERS OF THE FAITH (Philippians 1:7 KJV)

Philippians 1:7 Even as it is meet for me to think this of you all, because I have you in my heart; inasmuch as both in my bonds, and in the defence and confirmation of the gospel, ye all are partakers of my grace.

The apostle offers up thanksgivings and prayers, for the good work of grace in the Philippians. The highest honor of the most eminent ministers is, to be servants of Christ. And those who are not really saints on earth never will be saints in heaven. Out of Christ, the best saints are sinners, and unable to stand before God. There is no peace without grace. Inward peace springs from a sense of Divine favor. And there is no grace and peace but from God our Father, the fountain and origin of all blessings. At Philippi the apostle was evil entreated, and saw little fruit of his labor; yet he remembers Philippi with joy. We must thank our God for the graces and comforts, gifts and usefulness of others, as we receive the benefit, and God receives the glory. The work of grace will never be perfected till the day of Jesus Christ, the day of his appearance. But we may always be confident God will perform his good work, in every soul wherein he has really begun it by regeneration; though we must not trust in outward appearances, or in anything but a new creation to holiness. People are dear to their ministers, when they receive benefit by their ministry. Fellow-sufferers in the cause of God should be dear one to another. (Henry, 1706)

Called » ELDERS (1 Timothy 5:17; 1 Peter 5:1 KJV)
1 Timothy 5:17 Let the elders that rule well be counted worthy of double honour, especially they who labour in the word and doctrine.

Paul expresses great affection for Timothy. Care must be taken that ministers are maintained. And those who are laborious in this work are worthy of double honor and esteem. It is their just due, as much as the reward of the laborer. The apostle charges Timothy solemnly to guard against partiality. We have great need to watch at all times, that we do not partake of other men's sins. Keep thyself pure, not only from doing the like thyself, but from countenancing it, or any way helping to it in others. The apostle also charges Timothy to take care of his health. We are not to make our bodies masters, so neither slaves; but to use them so that they may be most helpful to us in the service of God. There are secret, and there are open sins: some men's sins are open before-hand, and going before unto judgment; some they follow after. God will bring to light the hidden things of darkness, and make known the counsels of all hearts. Looking forward to the judgment-day, let us all attend to our proper offices, whether in higher or lower stations, studying that the name and doctrine of God may never be blasphemed on our account. (Henry, 1706)

1 Peter 5:1 The elders which are among you I exhort, who am also an elder, and a witness of the sufferings of Christ, and also a partaker of the glory that shall be revealed:

But as making high pretences to liberty and purity. The apostle Peter does not command, but exhorts. He does not claim power to rule over all pastors and churches. It was the peculiar honor of Peter and a few more, to be witnesses of Christ's sufferings; but it is the privilege of all true Christians to partake of the glory that shall be revealed. These poor, dispersed, suffering Christians, were the flock of God, redeemed to God by the great Shepherd, living in holy love and communion, according to the will of God. They are also dignified with the title of God's heritage or clergy; his peculiar lot, chosen for his own people, to enjoy his special favor, and to do him special service. Christ is the chief Shepherd of the whole flock and heritage of God. And all faithful ministers will receive a crown of unfading glory, infinitely better and more honorable than all the authority, wealth, and pleasure of the world. (Henry, 1706)

Called » EVANGELISTS (Ephesians 4:11; 2 Timothy 4:5 KJV)
Ephesians 4:11 And he gave some, apostles; and some, prophets; and some, evangelists; and some, pastors and teachers;

To a due use of spiritual gifts and graces. Unto every believer is given some gift of grace, for their mutual help. All is given as seems best to Christ to bestow upon every one. He received for them, that he might give to them, a large measure of gifts and graces; particularly the gift of the Holy Ghost. Not a mere head knowledge, or bare acknowledging Christ to be the Son of God, but such as brings trust and obedience. There is a fullness in Christ and a measure of that fullness given in the counsel of God to every believer; but we never come to the perfect measure till we come to heaven. God's children are growing, as long as they are in this world; and the Christian's growth tends to the glory of Christ. The more a man finds himself drawn

out to improve in his station, and according to his measure, all that he has received, to the spiritual good of others, he may the more certainly believe that he has the grace of sincere love and charity rooted in his heart. (Henry, 1706)
2 Timothy 4:5 But watch thou in all things, endure afflictions, do the work of an evangelist, make full proof of thy ministry.

The apostle salutes Titus. People will turn away from the truth, they will grow weary of the plain gospel of Christ, they will be greedy

Call of Simon and others. When Christ began to preach, he began to gather disciples, who should be hearers, and afterwards preachers of his doctrine, who should be witnesses of his miracles, and afterwards testify concerning them. He went not to Herod's court, not to Jerusalem, among the chief priests and the elders, but to the Sea of Galilee, among the fishermen. The same power which called Peter and Andrew, could have wrought upon Annas and Caiaphas, for with God nothing is impossible. But Christ chooses the foolish things of the world to confound the wise. Diligence in an honest calling is pleasing to Christ, and it is no hindrance to a holy life. Idle people are more open to the temptations of Satan than to the calls of God. It is a happy and hopeful thing to see children careful of their parents, and dutiful. When Christ comes, it is good to be found doing. Am I in Christ? is a very needful question to ask ourselves; and, next to that, Am I in my calling? They had followed Christ before, as common disciples, John 1:37; now they must leave their calling. Those who would follow Christ aright, must, at his command, leave all things to follow him, must be ready to part with them. This instance of the power of the Lord Jesus encourages us to depend upon his grace. He speaks, and it is done. (Henry, 1706)

Mark 1:17 And Jesus said unto them, Come ye after me, and I will make you to become fishers of men.

Christ preaches and calls disciples. Jesus began to preach in Galilee, after that John was put in prison. If some be laid aside, others shall be raised up, to carry on the same work. Observe the great truths Christ preached. By repentance we give glory to our Creator whom we have offended; by faith we give glory to our Redeemer who came to save us from our sins. Christ has joined these two together, and let no man think to put them asunder. Christ puts honor upon those who, though mean in this world, are diligent in their business and kind to one another. Industry and unity are good and pleasant, and the Lord Jesus commands a blessing on them. Those, whom Christ calls, must leave all to follow him; and by his grace he makes them willing to do so. Not that we must needs go out of the world, but we must sit loose to the world; forsake everything that is against our duty to Christ, and that cannot be kept without hurt to our souls. Jesus strictly kept the Sabbath day, by applying himself unto, and abounding in the Sabbath work, in order to which the Sabbath rest was appointed. There is much in the doctrine of Christ that is astonishing; and the more we hear it, the more cause we see to admire it. (Henry, 1706)

Called » LABORERS (Matthew 9:38; with Philemon 1:1 KJV)

Matthew 9:38 Pray ye therefore the Lord of the harvest, that he will send forth labourers into his harvest.

He sends forth the apostles. Jesus visited not only the great and wealthy cities, but the poor, obscure villages; and there he preached, there he healed. The souls of the meanest in the world are as precious to Christ, and should be so to us, as the souls of those who make the greatest figure. There were priests, Levites, and scribes, all over the land; but they were idol shepherds, Zechariah 11:17;

therefore Christ had compassion on the people as sheep scattered, as men perishing for lack of knowledge. To this day vast multitudes are as sheep not having a shepherd, and we should have compassion and do all we can to help them. The multitudes desirous of spiritual instruction formed a plenteous harvest, needing many active laborers; but few deserved that character. Christ is the Lord of the harvest. Let us pray that many may be raised up and sent forth, who will labor in bringing souls to Christ. It is a sign that God is about to bestow some special mercy upon a people, when he stirs them up to pray for it. And commissions given to laborers in answer to prayer are most likely to be successful. (Henry, 1706)

Philemon 1:1 Paul, a prisoner of Jesus Christ, and Timothy our brother, unto Philemon our dearly beloved, and fellow laborers,

Paul's Greetings The significance of epistolary greetings goes beyond identifying author and audience; it is more than saying hello. The author's salutation, however conventional and formal, specifies the nature of the relationship between author and audience and even draws lines around the conversation being carried on by the letter in hand. Meanings are more readily and rightly determined in terms of this "rhetorical relationship" formulated by the letter's opening words. Thus, Philemon and the others mentioned in verse 2 hear the following request for Onesimus's restoration in terms of Paul, whose importance (and therefore the legitimacy of his appeal) is made clear by his opening self-introduction: the author is *a prisoner of Christ Jesus.* It is a claim so important to Paul's purpose that he repeats it thrice in the body of this very short letter (vv. 9, 13, 23). (Henry, 1706)

Paul's first audience is also made clear by his greeting. His address establishes an intimacy, even solidarity, with his readers--they are "dear brothers and sisters" and "coworkers and soldiers"--that can only increase the impact of his request and enhance the prospect of its compliance. And while it is true that Paul's salutation, found in verse 3, is rather conventional, it does present his essential understanding of what it means to belong to the church. He writes for the true Israel of God--an inclusive community called out of the world by the preaching of the gospel in order to bear witness to God's salvation within the world order (see commentary on Col 1:2). That is, the readers of Paul's letter must finally understand his subsequent request for Onesimus's restoration to reflect what it means to be the church and to do, as the church ought. The Author (1:1) (Henry, 1706)

Paul's introduction of himself is both similar and dissimilar to his Colossians greeting (Col 1:1-2). As before, he refers to Timothy as his co-writer (in some sense) and calls him *brother* (see commentary on Col 1:1). Unlike Colossians, where Paul cites his apostolic credentials to give his subsequent polemic greater legitimacy, he refers to himself here as *a prisoner of Christ Jesus,* thus introducing immediately an important motif for the rest of his letter (see introduction). Certainly, Paul intends to convey more than his historical situation (contra O'Brien 1983:271); in fact, he is not first of all a prisoner of Rome but a prisoner of Christ Jesus. His appellation interprets his literal imprisonment as a worshipful act--an act of devotion to Christ, of obedience to his calling. Paul does not appeal to his apostolic office (see vv. 8-10), not because it might offend his readership, close friends all (contra Melick 1991:348), but because the personal costs exacted by his imprisonment "allow him to speak to the community with greater authority" (Lohse 1971:189). (Henry, 1706)

The use of *prisoner* without the article is unusual and may suggest that Paul uses it as part of his proper name, which regularly is given without an article (Harris 1991:244). Since added names suggest the nature of a person's calling (Jesus is "Savior," Peter is "Rock"), Paul may well identify himself as Christ's prisoner to indicate the very substance of his missionary task and its costs. Further, he may be implying that the costliness of Christian ministry is the result of the revolutionary content of his message, thereby preparing Philemon for the revolutionary character of Paul's request of him. Paul's message bears witness to a new social order, and for that reason he finds himself in jail. This prepares us, then, for a radical word concerning the relations between a Roman slave and his owner. (Henry, 1706)

While Paul's imprisonment represents his missionary identity, it is Jesus for whom Paul is imprisoned. The response Paul strongly desires from Philemon springs from his orientation toward discipleship: because of Christ Jesus, Philemon should respond favorably toward Onesimus, even though it may be costly and at odds with the surrounding social order. The Audience (1: 1-2) (Henry, 1706)

Called » LABORERS IN THE GOSPEL OF CHRIST (1 Thessalonians 3:2 KJV) 1 Thessalonians 3:2 And sent Timotheus, our brother, and minister of God, and our fellowlabourer in the gospel of Christ, to establish you, and to comfort you concerning your faith:

The apostle sent Timothy to establish and comfort the Thessalonians. The more we find pleasure in the ways of God, the more we shall desire to persevere therein. The apostle's design was to establish and comfort the Thessalonians as to the object of their faith, that Jesus Christ was the Savior of the world; and as to the recompense of faith, which was more than enough to make up all their losses, and to reward all their labors. But he feared his labors would be in vain. If the devil cannot hinder ministers from laboring in the word and doctrine, he will, if possible, hinder the success of their labors. No one would willingly labor in vain. It is the will and purpose of God that we enter into his kingdom through many afflictions. And the apostles, far from flattering people with the expectation of worldly prosperity in religion, told them plainly they must count upon trouble in the flesh. Herein they followed the example of their great Master, the Author of our faith. Christians were in danger, and they should be forewarned; they will thus be kept from being improved by any devices of the tempter. (Henry, 1706)

Called » LIGHTS (John 5:35 KJV)

John 5:35 He was a burning and a shining light: and ye were willing for a season to rejoice in his light.

John 5:30-38

Our Lord returns to his declaration of the entire agreement between the Father and the Son, and declared himself the Son of God. He had higher testimony than that of John; his works bore witness to all he had said. But the Divine word had no abiding-place in their hearts, as they refused to believe in Him whom the Father had sent, according to his ancient promises. The voice of God, accompanied by the power of the Holy Ghost, thus made effectual to the conversion of sinners, still proclaims that this is the beloved Son, in whom the Father is well pleased. But when the hearts of men are full of pride, ambition, and the love of the world, there is no room for the word of God to abide in them. (Henry, 1706)

Called » MEN OF GOD (Deuteronomy 33:1; 1 Timothy 6:11 KJV)

Deuteronomy 33:1 And this is the blessing, wherewith Moses the man of God blessed the children of Israel before his death.

The glorious majesty of God. To all his precepts, warnings, and prophecies, Moses added a solemn blessing. He begins with a description of the glorious appearances of God, in giving the law. His law works like fire. If received, it is melting, warming, purifying, and burns up the dross of corruption; if rejected, it hardens, sears, pains, and destroys. The Holy Spirit came down in cloven tongues, as of fire; for the gospel also is a fiery law. The law of God written in the heart is a certain proof of the love of God shed abroad there: we must reckon His law one of the gifts of his grace. (Henry, 1706)

1 Timothy 6:11 But thou, O man of God, flee these things; and follow after righteousness, godliness, faith, love, patience, meekness.

The apostle exhorts Timothy to persevere with diligence, like a soldier, a combatant, and a husbandman. It ill becomes any men, but especially men of God, to set their hearts upon the things of this world; men of God should be taken up with the things of God. There must be a conflict with corruption, and temptations, and the powers of darkness. Eternal life is the crown proposed for our encouragement. We are called to lay hold thereon. To the rich must especially be pointed out their dangers and duties, as to the proper use of wealth. But who can give such a charge, that is not himself above the love of things that wealth can buy? The appearing of Christ is certain, but it is not for us to know the time. Mortal eyes cannot bear the brightness of the Divine glory. None can approach him except as he is made known unto sinners in and by Christ. The Godhead is here adored without distinction of Persons, as all these things are properly spoken, whether of the Father, the Son, or the Holy Ghost. God is revealed to us, only in and through the human nature of Christ, as the only begotten Son of the Father. (Henry, 1706)

Called » MESSENGERS OF THE CHURCH (2 Corinthians 8:23 KJV) fellowhelper concerning you: or our brethren be enquired of, they are the messengers of the churches, and the glory of Christ.

He recommends Titus to them. The apostle commends the brethren sent to collect their charity

2 Corinthians 8:23 Whether any do enquire of Titus, he is my partner and , that it might be known who they were, and how safely they might be trusted. It is the duty of all Christians to act prudently; to hinder, as far as we can, all unjust suspicions. It is needful, in the first place, to act uprightly in the sight of God, but things honest in the sight of men should also be attended to. A clear character, as well as a pure conscience, is requisite for usefulness. They brought glory to Christ as instruments, and had obtained honor from Christ to be counted faithful, and employed in his service. The good opinion others have of us, should be an argument with us to do well. (Henry, 1706)

Titus was a Greek and evidently a convert of Paul. The fact that Titus was not circumcised (Gal. 2:3) indicates that he had not been raised in Judaism nor had he become a proselyte. Paul highly esteemed Titus, who traveled with him to Jerusalem (Gal. 2:1-3) and served as his representative to the church at Corinth during Paul's third missionary journey (2 Cor. 7:6, 7; 8:6, 16). During this visit he delivered the letter known as 2 Corinthians to the believers there and urged them to contribute to Paul's offering for the poor in Jerusalem. He was later sent by Paul to Dalmatia (2 Tim. 4:10); Paul gave to Titus, a relatively young preacher of the gospel, the difficult assignment of directing the work in Crete. (New Spirit Filled Life® Bible, 2002)

"His speeches are really bad!" (2 Corinthians 10:10). That's what critics had to say about Paul, who more than any other person other than Jesus is responsible for starting Christianity. (Miller, 2004)

At least one other person in Paul's audience might have agreed—Eutychus, the young man who made the mistake of sitting on a high windowsill during one of Paul's all-night sermons. As lamplights flickered to the midnight hour, poor Eutychus "became very drowsy, finally, he sank

into a deep sleep and fell three stories to his death below"
(Acts 20:9)

Paul raises him from the dead, and then preached till
dawn.

He was like that. Not easily sidetracked.

That's the kind of man God chose to carry the Good News
about Jesus an estimated ten thousand miles from one end
of the Roman Empire to the other. A man who lumbered on
for some thirty years, refusing to give up even after three
shipwrecks, five beatings of thirty-nine lashes each, three
beatings with a roman rod, a public stoning that nearly
killed him, and no less than five imprisonments—probably
more.

God didn't need an eloquent talker.

He needed a relentless doer—someone who could stand up
to intolerant Jewish traditionalist.

He chose an intolerant Jewish traditionalist. (Miller, 2004)

The songwriter says, "Just ordinary people. My God
chooses plain old, ordinary people. He chooses people just
like you and me that are willing to do as He commands …"
Never underestimate the power of God to use you to do His
great work.

CHAPTER 5
SUMMARY AND CONCLUSIONS

Chaplains go where others would never consider! Never believe that a few kind and caring people cannot change the world. For in reality, they are the only ones who ever have. For example:

Chaplain James D. Johnson (2001) broke all the rules to be with his men. He chose to accompany them, unarmed, on their daily combat operations, a decision made against the recommendations of his superiors. During what would be the final days for some, he offered his ministry not from a pulpit but on the battlefields---in hot landing zones and rice paddies, in hospitals, aboard ship, and knee-deep in mud. He even found time for baptisms in the muddy Mekong River.

"You've never really lived until you've almost died," writes Johnson, one of the youngest army chaplains at the time. Through his compelling narration, he takes us into the hearts of frightened young boys and the minds of experienced men. In Combat Chaplain, we live for eight and one-half months with Johnson as he serves in the field with a small unit numbering 350 men. The physical price can be counted with numbers—ninety-six killed and over nine hundred wounded. Only those who paid it can understand the spiritual and psychological price, in a war that raised many difficult moral issues. "It placed my soul in the lost and found department for a while," Johnson writes. (Johnson, 2001)

Chaplain George Fox, a World War I hero, insisted on serving in World War II even though his wounds from the first conflict had not completely healed. (U.S. Army) (Kurzman, 2004)

Chaplain Alexander Goode enlisted in the army dreaming of a postwar world in which a feeling of universal brotherhood would find a "new era of humanity." (U.S.

Army) Goode was ordained a rabbi after several years of study while living in impoverishment. (Kurzman, 2004)

The poetry writing son of a famous evangelist, Chaplain Clark Poling thrived on challenges, whether on the football field or in the spiritual world, and like Moses, even tried once to speak with God atop a mountain. (U.S. Army) Young Clark Poling, along with his father, Minister Daniel A. Poling, and his brother, birth mother, and little sister were a closely knit family devoted to the welfare of others. Clark Poling became a prep school football star even though he weighed only 135 pounds. Clark Poling and his bride, Betty, together worked as one to lift their church from adversity to remarkable success. (Kurzman, 2004)

Chaplain John Washington, a priest from a struggling Irish family, who tricked the army into letting him serve by cheating on an eye test. (U.S. Army) A saintly image of John Washington in the window of St. Stephens Church in Kearny, New Jersey, expressing the sentiment of his parishioners toward him. (Kurzman, 2004)

The sinking of the troop carrier *Dorchester* in the icy waters off Greenland shortly after midnight on February 3, 1943, was one of the worst sea disasters of World War II. It was also the occasion of an astounding feat of heroism— and faith. (Kurzman, 2004)

As water gushed through a hole made by a German torpedo, four chaplains—members of different faiths but linked by bonds of friendship and devotion—moved quietly among the men on board. Preaching bravery, the chaplains distributed life jackets, including their own. In the end, these four men went down with the ship, their arms linked in spiritual solidarity, their voices raised in prayer. (Kurzman, 2004)

They were about as different as four American clergymen could be. George Lansing Fox (Methodist), wounded and decorated in World War I, loved his family and his Vermont congregation—yet he reenlisted as soon as he heard about Pearl Harbor. Rabbi Alex Goode was an athlete, an intellectual, and an adoring new father—yet he too knew, the day Pearl Harbor was bombed, that he would serve. Clark Poling (Dutch Reformed), the son of a famous radio evangelist, left for war begging his father to pray that he would never be a coward. Father John Washington (Catholic), a scrappy Irish street fighter, had dedicated himself to the church after a childhood brush with death. Despite their efforts to save as many of the nine hundred passengers as possible, two thirds died in the freezing water after a fatal command decision that delayed their rescue. (Kurzman, 2004)

As he left for his second tour of duty as an Army chaplain in Iraq, Roger Benimoff (2009) noted in his journal: *I am excited and I am scared. I am on fire for God. . . He is my hope, strength, and focus.* (Benimoff, 2009) Bur not long after returning to Iraq, the burdens of his job—the memorial services for soldiers killed in action, the therapy sessions after contact with the enemy, the perilous excursions "outside the wire" while under enemy fire— began to overwhelm him. Amid the dust, heat, and blood of Iraq, Benimof felt the pillar of strength he'd always relied on to hold him up—his faith in God—begin to crumble. (Benimoff, 2009)

Archaletta (1997) shares with us, in *God's Promises to His Children*, "The Scriptures can speak to us in whatever situation we are in. If we take the time to search them we can find the answer to all our daily problems. Whatever we are feeling, suffering or hoping.....the Bible has something to say to us. Let the Word of God speak to you now. As you read the following Promises of God I hope you will be uplifted and encouraged by them. May God Bless you as you read His Word! ..."He has given us His very great and precious promises..." 2 Peter 1:4 NIV

BELIEF

"I have come into the world as light, so that no one who believes in me should stay in darkness." John 12:46 NIV

"Yet to all who received him, to those who believed in his name, he gave the right to become children of God." John 1:12 NIV

CHARITY

"Give, and it will be given to you. A good measure, pressed down, shaken together and running over, will be poured into your lap." Luke 6:38 NIV

"A generous man will himself be blessed, for he shares his food with the poor." Proverbs 22:9 NIV

COMFORT

"God is our refuge and strength, an ever- present help in trouble." Psalm 46:1 NIV

"I have told you these things, so that in me you may have peace. In this world you will have trouble. But take heart! I have overcome the world! "John 16:33 NIV

"Come to me, all you who are weary and burdened, and I will give you rest." Matthew 11:28 NIV

COURAGE

"He gives strength to the weary and increases the power of the weak" Isaiah 40:29 NIV

"Fear not, for I have redeemed you; I have summoned you by name; you are mine" Isaiah 43:1b NIV

ETERNAL LIFE

"I tell you the truth, he who believes has everlasting life." John 6:47 NIV

"And this is what he promises us--even eternal life." 1 John 2:25 NIV

"Jesus said: 'I am the resurrection and the life. He who believes in me will live, even though he dies'....." John 11:25 NIV

"My sheep listen to my voice; I know them and they follow me. I give them eternal life, and they shall never perish; no one can snatch them out of my hand." John 10:27.28 NIV

FAITH
"Now faith is being sure of what we hope for and certain of what we do not see" Heb.11:1 NIV
"You are all sons of God through faith in Christ Jesus" Galatians 3:26 NIV
"We live by faith, not by sight" 2 Corinthians 5:7 NIV

FAITHFULNESS
"Know therefore that the Lord your God is God; he is the faithful God, keeping his covenant of love to a thousand generations of those who love him and keep his commands." Deuteronomy 7:9 NIV
"Though the mountains be shaken and the hills be moved, yet my unfailing love for you will not be shaken nor my covenant of peace be removed." Isaiah 54:10 NIV

GUIDANCE
"I will instruct you and teach you in the way you should go; I will counsel you and watch over you." Psalm 32:8 NIV
"I will lead the blind by ways they have not known, along unfamiliar paths I will guide them, I will turn the darkness into light before them and make the rough places smooth. These are the things I will do; I will not forsake them." Isaiah 42:16 NIV

JOY
"I have told you this so that my joy may be in you and your joy maybe complete" John 15

LONG LIFE
"Even to your old age and gray hairs I am he, I am he who will sustain you. I have made you and I will carry you; I will sustain you and I will rescue you. "Isaiah 46:4 NIV
"For through me your days will be many, and years will be added to your life." Proverbs 9:11 NIV

LOVE

"I have loved you with an everlasting love; I have drawn
you with loving-kindness." Jeremiah 31:3b NIV
"I love those who love me, and those who seek me find
me." Proverbs 8:17 NIV
"No eye has seen, no ear has heard, no mind has conceived
what

MERCY

"...the Lord longs to be gracious to you; he rises to show
you compassion. For the Lord is a God of justice. Blessed
are all who wait for him!" Isaiah 30:18 NIV
"As a father has compassion on his children, so the Lord
has compassion on those who fear him." Psalm 103:13 NIV

PEACE

"Peace I leave with you, my peace I give you. I do not give
as the world gives. Do not let your hearts be troubled and
do not be afraid." John 14:27 NIV
"And the peace of God, which transcends all
understanding, will guard your hearts and your minds in
Christ Jesus." Philippians 4:7

PRAYER

"Then you will call upon me and come and pray to me, and
I will listen to you." Jeremiah 29:12 NIV
"Before they call I will answer; while they are still
speaking I will hear." Isaiah 65:24 NIV
"This is the assurance we have in approaching God; that if
we ask anything according to his will, he hears us." 1 John
5:14 NIV

PROTECTION

"The Lord will keep you from all harm--he will watch over your life; the Lord will watch over your coming and going both now and forevermore." Psalm 121:7, 8 NIV

"When you pass through the waters, I will be with you; and when you pass through the rivers, they will not sweep over you. When you walk through the fire, you will not be burned; the flames will not set you ablaze." Isaiah 43:1, 2 NIV

"But whoever listens to me will live in safety and be at ease, without

SALVATION

"But when the kindness and love of God our Saviour appeared, he saved us, not because of righteous things we had done, but because of his mercy. He saved us through the washing of rebirth and renewal by the Holy Spirit, whom he poured out on us generously through Jesus Christ our Saviour." Titus 3:4-6 NIV

"Therefore, if anyone is in Christ, he is a new creation; the old has gone, the new has come!" 2 Corinthians 5:17 NIV

SUCCESS

"That everyone may eat and drink, and find satisfaction in all his toil--this is the gift of God." Ecclesiastes 3:13 NIV

"Moreover, when God gives any man wealth and possessions, and enables him to enjoy them, to accept his lot and be happy with his work---this is a gift of God." Ecclesiastes 5:19 NIV

"With me are riches and honor, enduring wealth and prosperity. My fruit is better than fine gold; what I yield surpasses choice silver." Proverbs 8: 18, 19 NIV

TRUST

"Trust in the Lord with all your heart and lean not on your own understanding; in all your ways acknowledge him, and he will make your paths straight." Proverbs 3:5, 6 NIV

"Blessed is the man who makes the Lord his trust...." Psalm 40:4a NIV

WISDOM
"For the Lord gives wisdom, and from his mouth come knowledge and understanding." Proverbs 2:6 NIV
".....He will teach us his ways, so that we may walk in his paths...." Isaiah 2:3 NIV

WORD OF GOD
"Fix these words of mine in your hearts and minds; tie them as symbols on your hands and bind them on your foreheads." Deuteronomy 11:18 NIV
"All scripture is God breathed and is useful for teaching, rebuking, correcting and training and righteousness." 2 Timothy 3:16 NIV
"Your word is a lamp to my feet and a light for my path." Psalm 119:105 NIV
"The word of God is living and active. Sharper than any double-edged sword, it penetrates even to dividing soul and spirit, joints and marrow; it judges the thoughts and attitudes of the heart." Hebrews 4:12 NIV
"Now I commit you to God and to the word of his grace, which can build you up and give you an inheritance among all those who are sanctified." Acts 20:32 NIV

"OUR THINKING vs. GOD'S PROMISES"
MAN/WOMAN: "It's impossible"
GOD: All things are possible (Luke18:27 KJV)
"And he said, The things which are impossible with men are possible with God."
MAN/WOMAN: "I'm too tired"
GOD: I will give you rest (Matthew 11:28-30 KJV)
"Come unto me, all ye that labour and are heavy laden, and I will give you rest. Take my yoke upon you, and learn

of me; for I am meek and lowly in heart: and ye shall find rest unto your souls. For my yoke is easy, and my burden is light. "

MAN/WOMAN: "Nobody really loves me"

GOD: I love you (John 2:16 & John 13:34 KJV)

"And said unto them that sold doves, Take these things hence; make not my Father's house an house of merchandise. "

"A new commandment I give unto you, That ye love one another; as I have loved you, that ye also love one another. "

MAN/WOMAN: "I can't go on"

GOD: My Grace is sufficient (II Corinthians 12:9 & Psalm 91:15 KJV)

"To another faith by the same Spirit; to another the gifts of healing by the same Spirit; "

"He shall call upon me, and I will answer him: I will be with him in trouble; I will deliver him, and honour him. "

MAN/WOMAN: "I can't figure things out"

GOD: I will direct your steps (Proverbs 3: 5-6 KJV)

"Trust in the LORD with all thine heart; and lean not unto thine own understanding. In all thy ways acknowledge him, and he shall direct thy paths. "

MAN/WOMAN: "I can't do it"

GOD: You can do all things (Philippians 4:13 KJV)

"I can do all things through Christ which strengtheneth me. "

MAN/WOMAN: "I'm not able"

GOD: I am able (II Corinthians 9:8 KJV)

"Say I these things as a man? or saith not the law the same also? "

MAN/WOMAN: "It's not worth it"

GOD: It will be worth it (Romans 8:28 KJV)

"And we know that all things work together for good to them that love God, to them who are the called according to his purpose. "

MAN/WOMAN: "I can't forgive myself"
GOD: I forgive you (I John 1:9 & Romans 8:1 KJV)
"If we confess our sins, he is faithful and just to forgive us our sins, and to cleanse us from all unrighteousness."
"There is therefore now no condemnation to them which are in Christ Jesus, who walk not after the flesh, but after the Spirit."
MAN/WOMAN: "I can't manage"
GOD: I will supply all your needs (Philippians 4:19 KJV)
"But my God shall supply all your need according to his riches in glory by Christ Jesus."
MAN/WOMAN: "I'm afraid"
GOD: I have not given you a spirit of fear (II Timothy 1:7 KJV)
"For God hath not given us the spirit of fear; but of power, and of love, and of a sound mind."
MAN/WOMAN: "I'm always worried and frustrated"
GOD: Cast all your cares on me (I Peter 5:7 KJV)
"Casting all your care upon him; for he careth for you."
MAN/WOMAN: "I don't have enough faith"
GOD: I've given everyone a measure of faith (Romans 12:3 KJV)
"For I say, through the grace given unto me, to every man that is among you, not to think of himself more highly than he ought to think; but to think soberly, according as God hath dealt to every man the measure of faith."
 MAN/WOMAN: "I'm not smart enough"
GOD: I give you wisdom (I Corinthians 1:30 KJV)
"But of him are ye in Christ Jesus, who of God is made unto us wisdom, and righteousness, and sanctification, and redemption:"
MAN/WOMAN: "I feel all alone"
God: I will never leave you or forsake you (Hebrews 13:5 KJV)

"Let your conversation be without covetousness; and be content with such things as ye have: for he hath said, I will never leave thee, nor forsake thee."

Levites are the descendants of Levi, one of the <u>Tribes Of Israel</u>, the <u>Children Of Jacob</u> (Genesis 29:34). The term is generally used, from the perspective of <u>The Bible</u>, to identify the part of the tribe that was set apart for the secondary duties of the sanctuary service (1 Kings 8:4, Ezra 2:70), as assistants to the priests, who were also Levites. Although all priests were Levites, not all Levites were priests.

Prior to the <u>Exodus</u>, when the Israelites escaped the slavery of the Pharaoh of Egypt (see <u>Who Was The Exodus Pharaoh?</u>), the ancient way of worship was yet observed, with the firstborn son of each household inheriting the priest's office. That was changed at Sinai (see <u>Wilderness Journey</u>) when a hereditary priesthood from the family of <u>Aaron</u> was established (Exodus 28:1).

The Levites were formally set apart after the now-infamous incident with the golden calf idol that the Israelites made while <u>Moses</u> was away receiving <u>The Ten Commandments</u> from The Lord (Exodus chapter 32). The Levites did not take part in the idolatry, and actually killed 3,000 of those who were running wild, as ordered by Moses (Exodus 32:25-29).

After the incident was over, Moses said of the Levites, "Today you have ordained yourselves for the service of The Lord, each one at the cost of his son and of his brother, that he may bestow a blessing upon you this day." (Exodus 32:29 ESV). The Levites were natural allies of Moses because Moses himself was of the tribe of Levi (Exodus 2:1-2, 10).

Levi had 3 sons - Gershon, Kohath, and Merari. From those branches of the family, the Levites were organized into 3 levels of service:

The first level was composed of Aaron and his offspring, who were descended from Levi's son Kohath. They formed the priesthood.

The second level was made up of all of the other descendants of Kohath who were not descendants of Aaron. They were in charge of the most sacred parts of the Tabernacle (Numbers 3:27-32, 4:4-15, 7:9).

The third level consisted of all of the descendants of Gershon and Merari, who were given lesser duties (Numbers 3:21-26, 33-37).

The Levites served at the Tabernacle from age 30 to 50 (Numbers 4:3, 23, 30). They were not counted for military service in the armies of Israel, but were set apart for service to God (Numbers 1:45-50, 2:33, 26:62).

Levites had custody of The Tabernacle (as illustrated above, see also What Happened To The Tabernacle?) (Numbers 1:51, 18:22-24). The Gershonites camped on the west of the Tabernacle (Numbers 3:23), the Kohathites on the south (Numbers 3:29), the Merarites on the north (Numbers 3:35), and the priests on the east (Numbers 3:38).

With their consecration to The Lord's service, the Levites were allotted no territorial inheritance of their own at the Division Of The Land; God was their inheritance (Numbers 18:20, 26:62, Deuteronomy 10:9). Once established in the Promised Land, they were supported, in the agricultural economy of the time, by the tithes of the produce of the land paid to The Lord by the other tribes.

The Levites were assigned towns to live in from the inheritance of the other tribes - forty-eight cities, thirteen of which were for the priests along with their other inhabitants (Numbers 35:2-5). Nine of these cities were in Judah, three in Naphtali, and four in each of the other tribes (Joshua chapter 21). Six of the Levitical cities were designated as Cities Of Refuge.

Deuteronomy 20:2-4 "And it shall be, when ye are come nigh unto the battle, that the priest shall approach and speak unto the people, And shall say unto them, Hear, O Israel, ye approach this day unto battle against your enemies: let not your hearts faint, fear not, and do not tremble, neither be ye terrified because of them; For the LORD your God is he that goeth with you, to fight for you against your enemies, to save you." (KJV)

Exhortation and proclamation respecting those who went to war.

In the wars wherein Israel engaged according to the will of God, they might expect the Divine assistance. The Lord was to be their only confidence. In these respects they were types of the Christian's warfare. Those unwilling to fight, must be sent away. The unwillingness might arise from a man's outward condition. God would not be served by men forced against their will. Thy people shall be willing, Ps 110:3. In running the Christian race, and fighting the good fight of faith, we must lay aside all that would make us unwilling. If a man's unwillingness rose from weakness and fear, he had leave to return from the war. The reason here given is, lest his brethren's heart fail as well as his heart. We must take heed that we fear not with the fear of them that are afraid, Isa 8:12. [Henry, 1706]

"In those days John the Baptist came, preaching in the desert of Judea and saying, "Repent, for the kingdom of heaven is near." This is he who was spoken of through the prophet Isaiah, "A voice of one calling in the desert, "Prepare the way for The Lord, make straight paths for Him." (Matthew 3:1-3 NIV)

John the Baptist is one of the best-known people of The Bible. And for good reason - he played a unique role in what, and Who, was to come. He was considered very highly by Jesus Christ, Who said about him, "Among those born of women there has not risen anyone greater than John the Baptist." (Matthew 11:11NIV). One certainly couldn't get a more rock-solid personal reference than that.

John was a prophet whose own coming was prophesied by an earlier prophet (see Prophecy) over 700 years before (Isaiah 40:3-5) - yet another illustration of God's step-by-step Plan.

John was a Levite. His father Zechariah was a Temple priest of the line of Abijah, and his mother Elizabeth was also descended from Aaron (Luke 1:5).

Jesus Christ and John the Baptist were related. Their mothers, Mary and Elizabeth, were cousins. (Luke 1:36). John the Baptist was born 6 months before Jesus Christ (Luke 1:36). He died about 6 months before Jesus Christ (Matthew 14:10-12).

The angel Gabriel separately announced the coming births of Jesus Christ and John the Baptist. John lived in the mountainous area of Judah, between Jerusalem and the Dead Sea (Matthew 3:1). "John's clothes were made of camel's hair (see Ships Of The Desert), and he had a leather belt around his waist. His food was locusts and wild honey." (Matthew 3:4 NIV).

John had a popular ministry. "People went out to him from Jerusalem and all Judea, and the whole region of The Jordan. Confessing their sins, they were baptized by him in the Jordan River (in photo above). (Matthew 3:5-6 NIV).

John the Baptist humbly baptized Jesus Christ (imagine the honor of being the one to do that). "Then Jesus came from Galilee to the Jordan to be baptized by John. But John tried to deter Him, saying, "I need to be baptized by You, and do You come to me? Jesus replied, "Let it be so now; it is proper for us to do this to fulfill all righteousness." (Matthew 3:13-15 NIV)

John's ministry became so popular that some wondered if he was the messiah. He answered, "I am not the Christ, but I am sent ahead of Him." (John 3:28 NIV). With the ministry of Jesus Christ then begun, John recognized that his own mission was nearing its end: "He must become greater; I must become less." (John 3:30 NIV)

John's ministry, and life, came to an end when he admonished Herod (see The Herods) for his sinful behavior (Luke 3:19-20). He was imprisoned at Machaerus, a fortress about 9 miles (15 kilometers) east of the Dead Sea. There, he was beheaded.

After he was killed, John's disciples came and buried his body, and then went and told Jesus all that had happened (Matthew 14:12). Jesus responded to the news of John's death by saying, "John was a lamp that burned and gave light, and you chose for a time to enjoy his light." (John 5:35 NIV)

If the witness of the Father is fundamental (5:32; cf. 1 John 5:9-12), what access do the Jewish opponents have to this testimony? There are four expressions of the Father's witness: the Baptist, Jesus' works Jesus' words and the Scripture. Each of these has been acknowledged earlier (1:35--2:22) as the basis of the disciples' faith (cf. von Wahlde 1981), and most of them will be developed further in later material: Jesus' works in 8:12-59, Jesus' words in 10:22-39 and the Scriptures in 6:30-59. The witness of John the Baptist is not developed further, but it is drawn upon again (10:40-41). (Henry, 1706)

John the Baptist (5:33-35), like Jesus, spoke what he heard from the Father (1:31-34). What he heard concerned Jesus, and so he bore witness to the truth; the truth is Christ (14:6). Not that Jesus had need of John's testimony (5:34). Jesus is one with the Father, so he has no need of human testimony for confirmation or help in knowing who he is. But the rest of us do have need of witnesses if we are to recognize him, so for our benefit he points out authentic witnesses. (Henry, 1706)

Specifically, he does so for the sake of these Jewish opponents' salvation (5:34), for divine grace motivates and characterizes all that he does. God desires that these opponents be saved, and so Jesus affirms the testimony of one whom the Jews themselves highly honored. John the Baptist was not the light (1:8), but he was at least a lamp (5:35). They rejoiced in his light but did not heed his teaching concerning Jesus. They failed to benefit from John. (Henry, 1706)

Suggestions for further research
This exploration is far from over! There are many facets of study that can be taken as suggested by the following questions:

Research Questions
What are the specific criteria on how to become a hospital, military, law enforcement, prison chaplain?
Who is a Chaplain?
What is the Chaplain Salary range?
When to call a chaplain?
When to Contact a Chaplain?
Why did you become a chaplain?
Can I volunteer as a Chaplain?
Will a chaplain accompany the Soldier who notifies the family of …?
Is it easy for a pastor to become a **chaplain**?
Can a VA **Chaplain** contact my civilian pastor/priest?
Should a retired navy chaplain wear his uniform when performing priestly duties?
Was Thomas Fuller a royal **chaplain**?
Is what I share with the staff and/or volunteer **chaplain** held in strict confidence?

Definitions
Belief
Function: *noun*

Etymology: Middle English *beleave,* probably alteration of Old English *gelēafa,* from *ge-,* associative prefix + *lēafa;* akin to Old English *lȳfan* — more at believe
Date: 12th century
1 : a state or habit of mind in which trust or confidence is placed in some person or thing
2 : something believed; *especially* : a tenet or body of tenets held by a group
3 : conviction of the truth of some statement or the reality of some being or phenomenon especially when based on examination of evidence

synonyms belief, faith, credence, credit mean assent to the truth of something offered for acceptance. belief may or may not imply certitude in the believer <my *belief* that I had caught all the errors>. faith almost always implies certitude even where there is no evidence or proof <an unshakable *faith* in God>. credence suggests intellectual assent without implying anything about grounds for assent <a theory now given *credence* by scientists>. credit may imply assent on grounds other than direct proof <gave full *credit* to the statement of a reputable witness>.

synonyms see in addition opinion (Merriam-Webster, 2010)

Charity
Main Entry: **char·i·ty**
Pronunciation: \'cher-ə-tē, 'cha-rə-\
Function: *noun*
Inflected Form(s): *plural* **char·i·ties**
Etymology: Middle English *charite,* from Anglo-French *charité,* from Late Latin *caritat-, caritas* Christian love, from Latin, dearness, from *carus* dear; akin to Old Irish *carae* friend, Sanskrit *kāma* love
Date: 13th century

1 : benevolent goodwill toward or love of humanity
2 a : generosity and helpfulness especially toward the needy or suffering; *also* **:** aid given to those in need **b :** an institution engaged in relief of the poor **c :** public provision for the relief of the needy
3 a : a gift for public benevolent purposes **b :** an institution (as a hospital) founded by such a gift
4 : lenient judgment of others

synonyms see mercy (Merriam-Webster, 2010)

Comfort
Main Entry: ¹**com·fort**
Pronunciation: \'kəm(p)-fərt\
Function: *transitive verb*
Etymology: Middle English, from Anglo-French *cunforter, comforter,* from Late Latin *confortare* to strengthen greatly, from Latin *com-* + *fortis* strong
Date: 13th century
1 : to give strength and hope to **:** cheer
2 : to ease the grief or trouble of **:** console (Merriam-Webster, 2010)

Courage
Main Entry: **cour·age**
Pronunciation: \'kər-ij, 'kə-rij\
Function: *noun*
Etymology: Middle English *corage,* from Anglo-French *curage,* from *quer, coer* heart, from Latin *cor* — more at heart
Date: 14th century
: mental or moral strength to venture, persevere, and withstand danger, fear, or difficulty

synonyms courage, mettle, spirit, resolution, tenacity mean mental or moral strength to resist opposition, danger, or hardship. <u>courage</u> implies firmness of mind and will in the face of danger or extreme difficulty <the *courage* to support unpopular causes>. <u>mettle</u> suggests an ingrained capacity for meeting strain or difficulty with fortitude and resilience <a challenge that will test your *mettle*>. <u>spirit</u> also suggests a quality of temperament enabling one to hold one's own or keep up one's morale when opposed or threatened <her *spirit* was unbroken by failure>. <u>resolution</u> stresses firm determination to achieve one's ends <the *resolution* of pioneer women>. <u>tenacity</u> adds to <u>resolution</u> implications of stubborn persistence and unwillingness to admit defeat <held to their beliefs with great *tenacity*> *(Merriam-Webster, 2010)*

Eternal life
This expression occurs in the Old Testament only in Dan. 12:2 (R.V., "everlasting life").
It occurs frequently in the New Testament (Matt. 7:14; 18:8, 9; Luke 10:28; comp. 18:18). It comprises the whole future of the redeemed (Luke 16:9), and is opposed to "eternal punishment" (Matt. 19:29; 25:46). It is the final reward and glory into which the children of God enter (1 Tim. 6:12, 19; Rom. 6:22; Gal. 6:8; 1 Tim. 1:16; Rom. 5:21); their Sabbath of rest (Heb. 4:9; comp. 12:22).
The newness of life which the believer derives from Christ (Rom. 6:4) is the very essence of salvation, and hence the life of glory or the eternal life must also be theirs (Rom. 6:8; 2 Tim. 2:11, 12; Rom. 5:17, 21; 8:30; Eph. 2:5, 6). It is the "gift of God in Jesus Christ our Lord" (Rom. 6:23). The life the faithful have here on earth (John 3:36; 5:24; 6:47, 53-58) is inseparably connected with the eternal life beyond, the endless life of the future, the happy future of the saints in heaven (Matt. 19:16, 29; 25:46). (Easton, 1897)

Faith
Main Entry: ¹**faith**
Pronunciation: \ˈfāth\
Function: *noun*
Inflected Form(s): *plural* **faiths** \ˈfāths, *sometimes* ˈfāth͟z\
Etymology: Middle English *feith,* from Anglo-French *feid, fei,* from Latin *fides;* akin to Latin *fidere* to trust — more at bide
Date: 13th century
1 a : allegiance to duty or a person : loyalty *b (1)* : fidelity to one's promises *(2)* : sincerity of intentions
2 a (1) : belief and trust in and loyalty to God *(2)* : belief in the traditional doctrines of a religion *b (1)* : firm belief in something for which there is no proof *(2)* : complete trust
3 : something that is believed especially with strong conviction; *especially* : a system of religious beliefs <the Protestant faith>
synonyms see belief
— **on faith :** without question <took everything he said *on faith*> (Merriam-Webster, 2010)

Faithfulness
Faithful
as a designation of Christians, means full of faith, trustful, and not simply trustworthy (Acts 10:45; 16:1; 2 Cor. 6:15; Col. 1:2; 1 Tim. 4:3, 12; 5:16; 6:2; Titus 1:6; Eph. 1:1; 1 Cor. 4:17, etc.).
It is used also of God's word or covenant as true and to be trusted (Ps. 119:86, 138; Isa. 25:1; 1 Tim. 1:15; Rev. 21:5; 22:6, etc.). (Easton, 1897)
Guidance
Main Entry: **guid·ance**
Pronunciation: \ˈgī-dᵊn(t)s\
Function: *noun*
Date: 1590

1 : the act or process of guiding
2 a : the direction provided by a guide **b** : advice on
vocational or educational problems given to students
3 : the process of controlling the course of a projectile by a
built-in mechanism (Merriam-Webster, 2010)

Joy
Main Entry: ¹**joy**
Pronunciation: \'jȯi\
Function: *noun*
Etymology: Middle English, from Anglo-French *joie,* from
Latin *gaudia,* plural of *gaudium,* from *gaudēre* to rejoice;
probably akin to Greek *gēthein* to rejoice
Date: 13th century
1 a : the emotion evoked by well-being, success, or good
fortune or by the prospect of possessing what one desires :
delight **b** : the expression or exhibition of such emotion :
gaiety
2 : a state of happiness or felicity : bliss
3 : a source or cause of delight
— **joy·less** \-ləs\ *adjective*
— **joy·less·ly** *adverb*
— **joy·less·ness** *noun* (Merriam-Webster, 2010)

Long life
Main Entry: **long–lived**
Pronunciation: \'lȯŋ-'livd *also* -'līvd\
Function: *adjective*
Date: 14th century
1 : having a long life : characterized by long life <a long–
lived family>
2 : lasting a long time : enduring (Merriam-Webster, 2010)

Love
Main Entry: ¹**love**
Pronunciation: \'ləv\

Function: *noun*
Etymology: Middle English, from Old English *lufu;* akin to Old High German *luba* love, Old English *lēof* dear, Latin *lubēre, libēre* to **please**
Date: before 12th century
1 a (1) : strong affection for another arising out of kinship or personal ties <maternal love for a <u>child</u> > *(2)* : attraction based on sexual desire : affection and tenderness felt by lovers *(3)* : affection based on admiration, benevolence, or common interests <love for his old schoolmates> **b** : an assurance of love <give her my love>
2 : warm attachment, enthusiasm, or devotion <love of the sea>
3 a : the object of attachment, devotion, or admiration <baseball was his first love> **b** *(1)* : a beloved person : <u>darling</u> —often used as a term of endearment *(2) British* — used as an informal term of address
4 a : unselfish loyal and benevolent concern for the good of another: as *(1)* : the fatherly concern of God for humankind *(2)* : brotherly concern for others **b** : a person's adoration of God
5 : a god or personification of love
6 : an amorous episode : <u>love affair</u>
7 : the sexual embrace : <u>copulation</u>
8 : a score of zero (as in tennis)
9 *capitalized Christian Science* : <u>god</u>
— **at love** : holding one's opponent scoreless in tennis
— **in love** : inspired by affection (Merriam-Webster, 2010)

Mercy
Main Entry: **mer·cy**
Pronunciation: \ˈmər-sē\
Function: *noun*
Inflected Form(s): *plural* **mercies**

Etymology: Middle English, from Anglo-French *merci,* from Medieval Latin *merced-, merces,* from Latin, price paid, wages, from *merc-, merx* merchandise
Date: 13th century
1 a : compassion or forbearance shown especially to an offender or to one subject to one's power; *also* : lenient or compassionate treatment <begged for mercy> **b :** imprisonment rather than death imposed as penalty for first-degree murder
2 a : a blessing that is an act of divine favor or compassion **b :** a fortunate circumstance <it was a mercy they found her before she froze>
3 : compassionate treatment of those in distress <works of mercy among the poor>
— **mercy** *adjective*
— **at the mercy of :** wholly in the power of : with no way to protect oneself against
synonyms mercy, charity, clemency, grace, leniency mean a disposition to show kindness or compassion. mercy implies compassion that forbears punishing even when justice demands it <threw himself on the *mercy* of the court>. charity stresses benevolence and goodwill shown in broad understanding and tolerance of others <show a little *charity* for the less fortunate>. clemency implies a mild or merciful disposition in one having the power or duty of punishing <the judge refused to show *clemency*>. grace implies a benign attitude and a willingness to grant favors or make concessions <by the *grace* of God>. leniency implies lack of severity in punishing <criticized the courts for excessive *leniency*>. (Merriam-Webster, 2010)

Peace
Main Entry: ¹**peace**
Pronunciation: \'pēs\
Function: *noun*

Etymology: Middle English *pees,* from Anglo-French *pes, pees,* from Latin *pac-, pax;* akin to Latin *pacisci* to agree — more at <u>pact</u>

Date: 12th century

1 : a state of tranquillity or quiet: as **a** : freedom from civil disturbance **b** : a state of security or order within a community provided for by law or custom <a breach of the peace>

2 : freedom from disquieting or oppressive thoughts or emotions

3 : harmony in personal relations

4 a : a state or period of mutual concord between governments **b** : a pact or agreement to end hostilities between those who have been at war or in a state of enmity

5 —used interjectionally to ask for silence or calm or as a greeting or farewell

— **at peace** : in a state of concord or tranquility (Merriam-Webster, 2010)

Prayer
Main Entry: **¹prayer**
Pronunciation: \'prer\
Function: *noun*
Usage: *often attributive*
Etymology: Middle English, from Anglo-French *priere, praiere, preiere,* from Medieval Latin *precaria,* from Latin, feminine of *precarius* obtained by entreaty, from *prec-, prex*

Date: 14th century

1 a (1) : an address (as a petition) to God or a god in word or thought <said a prayer for the success of the voyage> *(2)* : a set order of words used in praying **b** : an earnest request or wish

2 : the act or practice of praying to God or a god <kneeling in prayer>

3 : a religious service consisting chiefly of prayers —often

used in plural
4 : something prayed for
5 : a slight chance <haven't got a prayer> (Merriam-Webster, 2010)

Protection
Main Entry: **pro·tec·tion**
Pronunciation: \prə-ˈtek-shən\
Function: *noun*
Date: 14th century
1 : the act of <u>protecting</u> : the state of being <u>protected</u>
2 a : one that <u>protects</u> **b** : supervision or support of one that is smaller and weaker **c** : a <u>contraceptive</u> device (as a condom)
3 : the freeing of the producers of a country from foreign competition in their home market by restrictions (as high duties) on foreign competitive goods
4 a : immunity from prosecution purchased by criminals through bribery **b** : money extorted by racketeers posing as a <u>protective</u> association
5 : <u>coverage</u> 1a
6 : anchoring equipment placed in cracks for safety while rock climbing (Merriam-Webster, 2010)

Salvation
Main Entry: **sal·va·tion**
Pronunciation: \sal-ˈvā-shən\
Function: *noun*
Etymology: Middle English *salvacion,* from Anglo-French, from Late Latin *salvation-, salvatio,* from *salvare* to save — more at <u>save</u>
Date: 13th century
1 a : deliverance from the power and effects of sin **b** : the agent or means that effects salvation **c** *Christian Science* : the realization of the supremacy of infinite Mind over all bringing with it the destruction of the illusion of sin,

sickness, and death
2 : liberation from ignorance or illusion
3 a : preservation from destruction or failure **b :**
deliverance from danger or difficulty
— **sal·va·tion·al** \-shnəl, -shə-nᵊl\ *adjective* (Merriam-Webster, 2010)

Success
Main Entry: **suc·cess**
Pronunciation: \sək-ˈses\
Function: *noun*
Etymology: Latin *successus,* from *succedere*
Date: 1537
1 *obsolete* : <u>outcome</u>, <u>result</u>
2 a : degree or measure of succeeding **b :** favorable or
desired outcome; *also* : the attainment of wealth, favor, or
eminence
3 : one that succeeds (Merriam-Webster, 2010)

Trust
Main Entry: ¹**trust**
Pronunciation: \ˈtrəst\
Function: *noun*
Etymology: Middle English, probably of Scandinavian
origin; akin to Old Norse *traust* trust; akin to Old English
trēowe faithful — more at <u>true</u>
Date: 13th century
1 a : assured reliance on the character, ability, strength, or
truth of someone or something **b :** one in which confidence
is placed
2 a : dependence on something future or contingent : <u>hope</u>
b : reliance on future <u>payment</u> for property (as
merchandise) delivered : <u>credit</u> <bought furniture on trust>
3 a : a property interest held by one person for the <u>benefit</u>
of another **b :** a combination of firms or corporations
formed by a legal agreement; *especially* : one that reduces

or threatens to reduce competition
4 *archaic* **:** trustworthiness
5 *a (1)* **:** a charge or duty imposed in faith or confidence or as a condition of some relationship *(2)* **:** something committed or entrusted to one to be used or cared for in the interest of another **b :** responsible charge or office **c :** care, custody <the child committed to her trust>
— **in trust :** in the care or possession of a trustee (Merriam-Webster, 2010)

Wisdom
Main Entry: **wis·dom**
Pronunciation: \'wiz-dəm\
Function: *noun*
Etymology: Middle English, from Old English *wīsdōm,* from *wīs* wise
Date: before 12th century
1 a : accumulated philosophic or scientific learning : knowledge **b :** ability to discern inner qualities and relationships : insight **c :** good sense : judgment **d :** generally accepted belief <challenges what has become accepted wisdom among many historians — Robert Darnton>
2 : a wise attitude, belief, or course of action
3 : the teachings of the ancient wise men
synonyms see sense (Merriam-Webster, 2010)

Word of God
 (Heb. 4:12, etc.). The Bible so called because the writers of its several books were God's organs in communicating his will to men. It is his "word," because he speaks to us in its sacred pages. Whatever the inspired writers here declare to be true and binding upon us, God declares to be true and binding. This word is infallible, because written under the guidance of the Holy Spirit, and therefore free from all error of fact or doctrine or precept. (See INSPIRATION

◆T0001884; BIBLE ◆T0000580.) All saving knowledge is obtained from the word of God. In the case of adults it is an indispensable means of salvation, and is efficacious thereunto by the gracious influence of the Holy Spirit (John 17:17; 2 Tim. 3:15, 16; 1 Pet. 1:23). (Easton, 1897)

EPILOGUE

To think about especially with regard to taking action is the role of a chaplain. *Chaplains go where others would never consider!*

In the time of trouble or anxiety, to feel interest or concern and give a liking, fondness or the slightest inclination of being concerned about a person to the extent of doubtful or barely admissible care is priceless. *Never believe that a few kind and caring people cannot change the world.*

The essence of good-natured persons united by common traits or interests can change the world. *For in reality, they are the only ones who ever have.*

REFERENCES

Archaletta, Ed (1997) [Online] Retrieved March 17, 2010 from
http://www.smilegodlovesyou.org/promises.html

America's Navy - U.S. Government Web site operated by the United States Navy

Recruiting Command (1998) [Online] Retrieved March 17, 2010 from http://www.navy.com/careers/officer/chaplain/

Benimoff, R. with Conant, E. (2009) *Faith Under Fire (An Army Chaplain's Memoir)*.
New York: Crown Publishers.

Blank, Wayne (2002) John The Baptist [Online] Retrieved January 26, 2010 from
http://www.keyway.ca/htm2002/johnbapt.htm

Blank, Wayne (2002) Levites [Online] Retrieved January 26, 2010 from
http://www.keyway.ca/htm2002/levites.htm

Bowman III, G. W. (1998). *Dying, Grieving, Faith and Family (A Pastoral Approach)*.
New York: Haworth Pastoral Press.

Cart, J. (1995) "The Question About Monica," *Los Angeles Times*, May 28, 1995: C-1

Cart, J. (1995) "A Return To The Light," *Los Angeles Times*, August 18, 1995: C-1

Chaplain Manual (2007). Rules and Procedures Governing the Department Chaplain
Corps Los Angeles: W. Bratton, Chief, LAPD.

Crime In The United States, 2006 which contains the most current *Uniform Crime*
Reports date published by the U.S. Department of Justice, Federal Bureau of
Investigation.

Deisler, V. & Ambrose, M. (2008). *The Right Words for Any Occasion (The Complete*
Idiot's Guide). New York: Published by the Penguin Group.

Delaplane, David & Anne (2007) Victims of Child Abuse, Domestic Violence, Elder
Abuse, Rape, Robbery, Assault and Violent Death [Online] Retrieved March 16, 2010 from
http://www.ojp.usdoj.gov/ovc/publications/infores/clergy/transpar.htm
Easton, M. G. (1897) M.A., D.D., Illustrated Bible Dictionary, Third Edition, published by
Thomas Nelson, 1897. [Online] Retrieved June 6, 2010 from
http://www.biblegateway.com/resources/dictionaries/info.php
Foster, N. http://www.wisegeek.com/what_is_a_chaplain.htm. Website written by Nikki
Foster Copyright 2003-2009. Congesture Corporation.
Getz, G. (2002). Encouraging One Another. Colorado Springs: Victor Books is an
imprint of Cook Communications Ministries.
Gibson, Donald (1996-2010) Chaplain Fellowship Ministries [Online] Retrieved March
        18, 2010 from http://www.chaplain-ministries.com/
Johnson, J. D. (2001). Combat Chaplain (A Thirty-Year Vietnam Battle). Texas:
University of North Texas Press.
Henry, Matthew (1706) Matthew Henry's Concise Commentary on the Bible is available
in the Public Domain.
Hyams, Wignall & Roswell (1996) "War Syndromes and Their Evaluation: From The
U.S. Civil War To the Persian Gulf War." *Annals of Internal Medicine* V125, N5
September 1996: 398-405
Kates, A. R. (2008). *CopShock*. Tucson: Holbrook Street Press.
Kirkpatrick, C. (1995) "Monica's Dark Odyssey," *Newsweek*, September 4, 1995: 48-49

Kobrick, F.R. "Reaction of Vietnam Veterans to the Persian Gulf War," *Health & Social Work*, V18, N3, 1993: p. 166

Kruitsinger, J. (2001). Peace Officers for Christ International. Peacemakers Journal. Santa Ana, California – Santa Ana Police Department.

Kurzman, D. (2004). *No Greater Glory*. USA: Random House.

Landsberg, M., (1995) "World War II Ghosts Come Back To Haunt Veterans 50 Years Later," Associated Press, August 6, 1995: A-1.

Liberty University. (1988). The King James Study Bible. Nashville: Thomas Nelson Publishers.

Marine Corp Reference Publication (MCRP) 6-12A (2003) *Religious Ministry Team Handbook* Department of the Navy Headquarters USMC Washington, DC.

Hanson, Edward, Jr. Lieutenant General, USMC Commanding General

Matsakis, A. (n.d.) *I Can't Get Over It, A Handbook For Trauma Survivors, Second Edition*, p.14.

Merriam-Webster Online Dictionary (2010) In *Merriam-Webster Online Dictionary*. Retrieved June 6, 2010, from http://www.merriam-webster.com/dictionary/

Miller, Stephen M. (2004). *Who's Who and Where's Where in the Bible*. Barbour Publishing, Inc.

Norman, J. (2004) Retrieved (n.d.) from http://en.wikipedia.org/wiki/Chaplain

Simon & Schuster, Inc. (1991). Webster's New World Dictionary. New York: Prentice Hall.

Paget, N. & McCormack, J. (2006) *The Work of the Chaplain*. Valley Forge: Judson Press.

Solomon, S.D., Davidson, J.R. "Trauma: Prevalence, Impairment, Service Use and Cost," *Journal of Clinical Psychiatry*, V58, Suppl., N9, 1997: 5-11.

Switzer, D. K. (1989) *Pastoral Care Emergencies (Ministering to People in Crisis)*.
        New York: Laulist Press.

The Zondervan Corporation. (1995-2009) All Rights Reserved. [Online] Retrieved March 17, 2010 from http://www.biblegateway.com/topical/topical_searchresults.php?source=1&seahtype=all&search=strength&offset=0&resultspp=25

Warren, R. (2002). *The Purpose Driven Life*. Grand Rapids: Zondervan.

APPENDIX A
GLOSSARY
A

Academy a secondary school (usually private) - a secondary school (usually private)...

Address (computer science) the code that identifies where a piece of information is stored - (computer science) the code that identifies where a piece of information is stored...

Adultery extramarital sex that willfully and maliciously interferes with marriage relations; "adultery is often cited as grounds for divorce" - extramarital sex that willfully and maliciously interferes with marriage relations; "adultery is often cited as grounds for divorce"...

After located farther aft - located farther aft...

Aides (Greek mythology) the god of the underworld in ancient mythology; brother of Zeus and husband of Persephone - (Greek mythology) the god of the underworld in ancient mythology; brother of Zeus and husband of Persephone...

Assisting give help or assistance; be of service; "everyone helped out during the earthquake"; "can you help me carry this table?"; "she never helps around the house" - give help or assistance; be of service; "everyone helped out during the earthquake"; "can you help me carry this table?"; "she never helps around the house" ...

B

Biographical of or relating to or being biography; "biographical data" - of or relating to or being biography; "biographical data"...

Black the quality or state of the achromatic color of least lightness (bearing the least resemblance to white) - the quality or state of the achromatic color of least lightness (bearing the least resemblance to white)...

Bumper a glass filled to the brim (especially as a toast); "we quaffed a bumper of ale" - a glass filled to the brim (especially as a toast); "we quaffed a bumper of ale"...

C

Called assign a specified (usually proper) proper name to; "they named their son David"; "the new school was named after the famous civil rights leader" - assign a specified (usually proper) proper name to; "they named their son David"; "the new school was named after the famous civil rights leader" ...

Cap a tight-fitting headdress - a tight-fitting headdress...

Career the particular occupation for which you are trained - the particular occupation for which you are trained...

Centenary the 100th anniversary (or the celebration of it) - the 100th anniversary (or the celebration of it)...

Change an event that occurs when something passes from one state or phase to another; "the change was intended to increase sales"; "this storm is certainly a change for the worse"; "the neighborhood had undergone few modifications since his last visit years ago" - an event that occurs when something passes from one state or phase to another; "the change was intended to increase sales"; "this storm is certainly a change for the worse"; "the neighborhood had undergone few modifications since his last visit years ago" ...

Chap a boy or man; "that chap is your host"; "there's a fellow at the door"; "he's a likable cuss" - a boy or man; "that chap is your host"; "there's a fellow at the door"; "he's a likable cuss"...

Chaplaincy the position of chaplain - the position of chaplain...

Chaps a boy or man; "that chap is your host"; "there's a fellow at the door"; "he's a likable cuss" - a boy or man; "that chap is your host"; "there's a fellow at the door"; "he's a likable cuss"...

Clinical relating to a clinic or conducted in or as if in a clinic and depending on direct observation of patients; "clinical observation"; "clinical case study" - relating to a clinic or conducted in or as if in a clinic and depending on

direct observation of patients; "clinical observation";
"clinical case study" ...
Created make or cause to be or to become; "make a mess in
one's office"; "create a furor" - make or cause to be or to
become; "make a mess in one's office"; "create a furor" ...
D
Dayton a city in southwest Ohio; manufacturing center - a
city in southwest Ohio; manufacturing center...
Decried express strong disapproval of; "we condemn the
racism in south Africa"; "these ideas were reprobated" -
express strong disapproval of; "we condemn the racism in
south Africa"; "these ideas were reprobated" ...
Depending be contingent upon (something that is elided);
"that depends" - be contingent upon (something that is
elided); "that depends"...
Descriptions a statement that represents something in
words - a statement that represents something in words...
Devil (Judeo-Christian and Islamic religions) chief spirit of
evil and adversary of god; tempter of mankind; master of
hell - (Judeo-Christian and Islamic religions) chief spirit of
evil and adversary of god; tempter of mankind; master of
hell...
E
Entertainment an activity that is diverting and that holds the
attention - an activity that is diverting and that holds the
attention...
F
Fall the season when the leaves fall from the trees; "in the
fall of 1973" - the season when the leaves fall from the
trees; "in the fall of 1973"...
Feelings emotional or moral sensitivity (especially in
relation to personal principles or dignity); "the remark hurt
his feelings" - emotional or moral sensitivity (especially in
relation to personal principles or dignity); "the remark hurt
his feelings"...

Fellowship an association of people who share common beliefs or activities; "the message was addressed not just to employees but to every member of the company family"; "the church welcomed new members into its fellowship" - an association of people who share common beliefs or activities; "the message was addressed not just to employees but to every member of the company family"; "the church welcomed new members into its fellowship" ...

Filled make full, also in a metaphorical sense; "fill a container"; "fill the child with pride" - make full, also in a metaphorical sense; "fill a container"; "fill the child with pride" ...

Fort a fortified military post where troops are stationed - a fortified military post where troops are stationed...

G

Great a person who has achieved distinction and honor in some field; "he is one of the greats of American music" - a person who has achieved distinction and honor in some field; "he is one of the greats of American music"...

Greeting (usually plural) an acknowledgment or expression of good will (especially on meeting) - (usually plural) an acknowledgment or expression of good will (especially on meeting)...

Groups any number of entities (members) considered as a unit - any number of entities (members) considered as a unit...

Guidance something that provides direction or advice as to a decision or course of action - something that provides direction or advice as to a decision or course of action...

H

Hall an interior passage or corridor onto which rooms open; "the elevators were at the end of the hall" - an interior passage or corridor onto which rooms open; "the elevators were at the end of the hall"...

Household a social unit living together; "he moved his family to Virginia"; "it was a good Christian household"; "I

waited until the whole house was asleep"; "the teacher
asked how many people made up his home" - a social unit
living together; "he moved his family to Virginia"; "it was a
good Christian household"; "I waited until the whole house
was asleep"; "the teacher asked how many people made up
his home"...

I

Illness impairment of normal physiological function
affecting part or all of an organism - impairment of normal
physiological function affecting part or all of an organism...
Inc a heterogeneous collection of groups united in their
opposition to Saddam Hussein's government of Iraq;
formed in 1992 it is comprised of Sunni and Shiite Arabs
and Kurds who hope to build a new government - a
heterogeneous collection of groups united in their
opposition to Saddam Hussein's government of Iraq;
formed in 1992 it is comprised of Sunni and Shiite Arabs
and Kurds who hope to build a new government...
Includes have as a part, be made up out of; "the list
includes the names of many famous writers" - have as a
part, be made up out of; "the list includes the names of
many famous writers"...

L

Leader a person who rules or guides or inspires others - a
person who rules or guides or inspires others...
Leadership the activity of leading; "his leadership inspired
the team" - the activity of leading; "his leadership inspired
the team"...
Learning the cognitive process of acquiring skill or
knowledge; "the child's acquisition of language" - the
cognitive process of acquiring skill or knowledge; "the
child's acquisition of language"...
Lot(often followed by `of') a large number or amount or
extent; "a batch of letters"; "a deal of trouble"; "a lot of
money"; "he made a mint on the stock market"; "it must
have cost plenty" - (often followed by `of') a large number

or amount or extent; "a batch of letters"; "a deal of trouble";
"a lot of money"; "he made a mint on the stock market"; "it
must have cost plenty" ...

M

Major a commissioned military officer in the united states
army or air force or marines; below lieutenant colonel and
above captain - a commissioned military officer in the
united states army or air force or marines; below lieutenant
colonel and above captain ...

Marriage the state of being a married couple voluntarily
joined for life (or until divorce); "a long and happy
marriage"; "God bless this union" - the state of being a
married couple voluntarily joined for life (or until divorce);
"a long and happy marriage"; "God bless this union"...

Media a means or instrumentality for storing or
communicating information - a means or instrumentality
for storing or communicating information...

Military the military forces of a nation; "their military is the
largest in the region"; "the military machine is the same one
we faced in 1991 but now it is weaker" - the military forces
of a nation; "their military is the largest in the region"; "the
military machine is the same one we faced in 1991 but now
it is weaker"...

Mission an organization of missionaries in a foreign land
sent to carry on religious work - an organization of
missionaries in a foreign land sent to carry on religious
work...

N

Needs a condition requiring relief; "she satisfied his need
for affection"; "god has no need of men to accomplish his
work"; "there is a demand for jobs" - a condition requiring
relief; "she satisfied his need for affection"; "god has no
need of men to accomplish his work"; "there is a demand
for jobs" ...

Needy people collectively; "they try to help the needy" -
needy people collectively; "they try to help the needy"...

<u>Next</u> nearest in space or position; immediately adjoining without intervening space; "had adjacent rooms"; "in the next room"; "the person sitting next to me"; "our rooms were side by side" - nearest in space or position; immediately adjoining without intervening space; "had adjacent rooms"; "in the next room"; "the person sitting next to me"; "our rooms were side by side" <u>...</u>

O

<u>Office</u> place of business where professional or clerical duties are performed; "he rented an office in the new building" - place of business where professional or clerical duties are performed; "he rented an office in the new building"<u>...</u>

<u>Ohio</u> a Midwestern state in north central united states in the great lakes region - a Midwestern state in north central united states in the great lakes region <u>...</u>

<u>Opening</u> an open or empty space in or between things; "there was a small opening between the trees"; "the explosion made a gap in the wall" - an open or empty space in or between things; "there was a small opening between the trees"; "the explosion made a gap in the wall"<u>...</u>

<u>Organizations</u> a group of people who work together - a group of people who work together<u>...</u>

<u>Outpatient</u> a patient who does not reside in the hospital where he is being treated - a patient who does not reside in the hospital where he is being treated<u>...</u>

P

<u>Pain</u> a symptom of some physical hurt or disorder; "the patient developed severe pain and distension" - a symptom of some physical hurt or disorder; "the patient developed severe pain and distension"<u>...</u>

<u>Partners</u> a person's partner in marriage - a person's partner in marriage<u>...</u>

<u>Pastoral</u> a musical composition that evokes rural life - a musical composition that evokes rural life<u>...</u>

Peter disciple of Jesus and leader of the apostles; regarded by Catholics as the vicar of Christ on earth and first pope - disciple of Jesus and leader of the apostles; regarded by Catholics as the vicar of Christ on earth and first pope...
Philip Englishman and husband of Elizabeth ii (born 1921) - Englishman and husband of Elizabeth ii (born 1921)...
Post the position where someone (as a guard or sentry) stands or is assigned to stand; "a soldier manned the entrance post"; "a sentry station" - the position where someone (as a guard or sentry) stands or is assigned to stand; "a soldier manned the entrance post"; "a sentry station"...
Profile an analysis (often in graphical form) representing the extent to which something exhibits various characteristics; "a biochemical profile of blood"; "a psychological profile of serial killers" - an analysis (often in graphical form) representing the extent to which something exhibits various characteristics; "a biochemical profile of blood"; "a psychological profile of serial killers"
...

Q
Qualify prove capable or fit; meet requirements - prove capable or fit; meet requirements...

R
Receive get something; come into possession of; "receive payment"; "receive a gift"; "receive letters from the front" - get something; come into possession of; "receive payment"; "receive a gift"; "receive letters from the front" ...
Reestablished bring back into original existence, use, function, or position; "restore law and order"; "reestablish peace in the region"; "restore the emperor to the throne" - bring back into original existence, use, function, or position; "restore law and order"; "reestablish peace in the region"; "restore the emperor to the throne" ...
Related make a logical or causal connection; "I cannot connect these two pieces of evidence in my mind";

"colligate these facts"; "I cannot relate these events at all" -
make a logical or causal connection; "I cannot connect
these two pieces of evidence in my mind"; "colligate these
facts"; "I cannot relate these events at all" ...
Represent take the place of or be parallel or equivalent to;
"because of the sound changes in the course of history, an
'h' in Greek stands for an 's' in Latin" - take the place of or
be parallel or equivalent to; "because of the sound changes
in the course of history, an 'h' in Greek stands for an 's' in
Latin"...
Rights an abstract idea of that which is due to a person or
governmental body by law or tradition or nature; "they are
endowed by their creator with certain unalienable rights";
"certain rights can never be granted to the government but
must be kept in the hands of the people"- Eleanor
Roosevelt; "a right is not something that somebody gives
you; it is something that nobody can take away" - an
abstract idea of that which is due to a person or
governmental body by law or tradition or nature; "they are
endowed by their creator with certain unalienable rights";
"certain rights can never be granted to the government but
must be kept in the hands of the people"- Eleanor
Roosevelt; "a right is not something that somebody gives
you; it is something that nobody can take away" ...
Royal a sail set next above the topgallant on a royal mast -
a sail set next above the topgallant on a royal mast...
S
Senator a member of a senate - a member of a senate...
Sept the month following august and preceding October -
the month following august and preceding October...
Sieges the action of an armed force that surrounds a
fortified place and isolates it while continuing to attack -
the action of an armed force that surrounds a fortified place
and isolates it while continuing to attack...
Specific a fact about some part (as opposed to general); "he
always reasons from the particular to the general" - a fact

about some part (as opposed to general); "he always
reasons from the particular to the general"...

<u>Speech</u> the act of delivering a formal spoken
communication to an audience; "he listened to an address
on minor roman poets" - the act of delivering a formal
spoken communication to an audience; "he listened to an
address on minor roman poets" ...

<u>Squad</u> a smallest army unit - a smallest army unit...

<u>Start</u> the beginning of anything; "it was off to a good start"
- the beginning of anything; "it was off to a good start"...

<u>Strategy</u> an elaborate and systematic plan of action - an
elaborate and systematic plan of action...

<u>Student</u> a learner who is enrolled in an educational
institution - a learner who is enrolled in an educational
institution...

<u>Students</u> a learner who is enrolled in an educational
institution - a learner who is enrolled in an educational
institution...

<u>Sundays</u> first day of the week; observed as a day of rest and
worship by most Christians - first day of the week;
observed as a day of rest and worship by most Christians...

<u>Supervise</u> watch and direct; "who is overseeing this
project?" - watch and direct; "who is overseeing this
project?"...

T

Talk an exchange of ideas via conversation; "let's have
more work and less talk around here" - an exchange of
ideas via conversation; "let's have more work and less talk
around here"...

Tasks any piece of work that is undertaken or attempted;
"he prepared for great undertakings" - any piece of work
that is undertaken or attempted; "he prepared for great
undertakings"...

V

Virtual being actually such in almost every respect; "a
practical failure"; "the once elegant temple lay in virtual
ruin" - being actually such in almost every respect; "a
practical failure"; "the once elegant temple lay in virtual
ruin"...

W

Wesleyan a follower of Wesleyanism - a follower of
Wesleyanism...

Wing a movable organ for flying (one of a pair) - a
movable organ for flying (one of a pair) ...

Wink a very short time (as the time it takes the eye blink or
the heart to beat); "if I had the chance I'd do it in a flash" -
a very short time (as the time it takes the eye blink or the
heart to beat); "if I had the chance I'd do it in a flash"...

APPENDIX B

riped necessitate bill, "Nolan Bill" in 1978, this bill that Pat Nolan, reserve officer levels

aided for designated line reserve the same as full-embards, noting first large police said their new ates to this post-

1980s, Newton shot reserve program. Reserve Officer reserves would Z-units, then as

March 1, 1983; and G.B. Mogle of 77th Division, who was shot by a prowler suspect on July 31, 1946. Mogle, whose story was nearly lost, succumbed to his wounds a week later on August 7, 1946. The suspect was captured five days later.

Reserves Today

Our current 700-plus active reserve officers have volunteered more than 200,000 hours of service to their communities. They work a variety of assignments, including Patrol, Air Support, Bicycle Detail, Mounted Unit, Bomb Squad and Firearms. Reserves come from all walks of life, who in their 9-to-5 lives work as doctors, Hollywood entertainers, pilots, business owners, homemakers, teachers and even councilmembers. "What [reserves] all have in common is an irresistible sense of duty to give back to society and a calling to be more than a spectator in life," says Councilmen Greig Smith, who is a current reserve. The exact standards to become a reserve officer match those of regular officers,

yosa with LAPD Reserve Motor officers at nal Parade: from left, Officers Larry Rowland, loore, Jeff Nocket and Gary Becker. Reserve y detail for the event.

sher as A-units." verof, the LAPD qualified reserves shed Designated scentially allowed to work in spe-ling Crash/SPU. mo. Air Support. lemonism and as

r 1980s, LAPD erve program in support services as desk, commu-

he continues.

"It's truly 'community policing,' exemplified by the motto of the program: To be a reserve is to be twice a citizen," says Smith.

As Officer in Charge of the Reserve Officer and Volunteer Section, Lieutenant **Craig Herron** oversees day-to-day operations of the reserve corps, including auditing the program.

Despite a wrecked economy, according to Herron, reserve numbers have continued rising with some looking into full-time commitment. "Although many

The Chief with reserve officers of the year: Rampart's Fernando Macias, Northeast's Catherine Euler, Central's Wilson Roth, Newton's Reverend Richard McCready, Newton's Dr. Alfredo Noble and Central Traffic's Mario Escobar.

Pacific's co-bureau reserve officers of the year Martin Greenblatt and Patricia Smiley with reserve officers of the year: Wilshire's Alton Jones, WLA's Ken Alridge, West Traffic's Todd Moore and Olympic's Max Kerstein.

are facing economic hardship, they continue to provide the same outstanding service to the citizens of Los Angeles and the Department, just as they did in better economic times," says Herron, noting that today's reserves are working in almost every division of the city.

Reserve Associate Membership

The Los Angeles Police Protective League offers reserves an opportunity to become Associate members. For more information, please refer to Director Corina Lee's article on page 4.

Twice a Citizen

The Los Angeles Police Reserve Foundation is a philanthropic group that supports training and equipment, as well as reserve activities like the Special Olympics summer games and Sunshine Kids, bereavement assistance and reserve Motor Unit.

The foundation hosts an annual Twice a Citizen Awards banquet, which raises funds for the reserve foundation

Lombardi – both level-one reserves "The primary use of this banquet i to honor our reserves who have been extraordinary throughout the year," say Herron, adding forthrightly that, "the do just about everything that a full-tim officer does." ❖

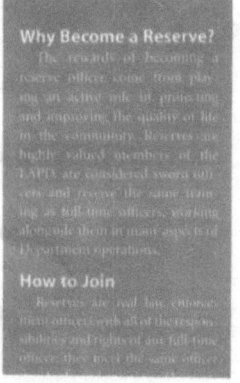

Why Become a Reserve?

The rewards of becoming a reserve officer come from play ing an active role in protecting and improving the quality of life in the community. Reserves are highly valued members of the LAPD, are considered sworn offi cers and receive the same train ing as full-time officers, working alongside them in many aspects of Department operations.

How to Join

Reserves are real law enforce ment officers with all of the respon sibilities and rights of any full-time officer; they meet the same offic

City of Los Angeles

CERTIFICATE OF APPRECIATION

is hereby presented by

COUNCILMAN GILBERT W. LINDSAY
NINTH COUNCIL DISTRICT

to

REVEREND

Richard McCready

IN RECOGNITION *of outstanding and dedicated service to the community and the City of Los Angeles.*

CURRICULUM VITA

When Clara and I were married in 1959, we were not dedicated Christians. Both of us expected to enjoy a fulfilling marriage and a rich family life. We didn't have any reason to think otherwise.

"Let thy fountain be blessed: and rejoice with the wife of thy youth." (Proverbs 5:18)

But as the years went along, we began to become disillusioned.   We completed our education and plunged into pastor our first church. Over the next several years, our children were born. To the outward appearance, our life was very good. The truth was that we were struggling.

"Judge not according to the appearance, but judge righteous judgment." (John 7:24)

By the time we had been married ten or twelve years. We had become two strong-willed personalities of the object sex who lived in the same house. We shared with the children, and had the same basic spiritual views and values. But, we disagreed on almost everything else.

"Can two walk together, except they be agreed?" (Amos 3:3)

I got a job with the City where I worked 36 years until retiring as pastor and all. I believe God made ways for us. I do believe God helped us through our marriage. We have been married fifty years and I am yet married to the same woman. Our children are grown and doing very well.

"If any be blameless, the husband of one wife, having faithful children not accused of riot or unruly." (Titus 1:6)
Something was missing and we didn't know what it was. Like many others, we found that we could always exemplify the Christian life when we were away from home, because difficulties come in shorter and less pressure doses. But at home where our real selves come out; the pressure was too intense clearly, knowing what marriage and family life was supposed to look like wasn't the "us" understanding how to live it. God knew we needed His help more than we knew it.

"Therefore judge nothing before the time, until the Lord come, who both will bring to light the hidden things of darkness, and will make manifest the counsels of the hearts: and then shall every man have praise of God." (1 Corinthians 4:5)
So in 1964 we encountered the power of the Holy Ghost. Our lives have never been the same since then. He worked with us we raised our children.

"But ye shall receive power, after that the Holy Ghost is come upon you: and ye shall be witnesses unto me both in Jerusalem, and in all Judaea, and in Samaria, and unto the uttermost part of the earth." (Acts 1:8)
Gradually as we yielded control to God; control of our selfishness, our anger, fears, and all. God replaced them with joy and peace.

"I speak after the manner of men because of the infirmity of your flesh: for as ye have yielded your members servants to uncleanness and to iniquity unto iniquity; even so now yield your members servants to righteousness unto holiness." (Romans 6:19)